brilliant

stress
management

How to manage stress in any situation

Mike Clayton

Prentice Hall
is an imprint of

Harlow, England • London • New York • Boston • San Francisco • Toronto • Sydney • Singapore • Hong Kong
Tokyo • Seoul • Taipei • New Delhi • Cape Town • Madrid • Mexico City • Amsterdam • Munich • Paris • Milan

PEARSON EDUCATION LIMITED
Edinburgh Gate
Harlow CM20 2JE
Tel: +44 (0)1279 623623
Fax: +44 (0)1279 431059
Website: www.pearson.com/uk

First published in Great Britain in 2011

Pearson Education is not responsible for the content of third-party internet sites.

ISBN: 978-0-273-75054-3

British Library Cataloguing-in-Publication Data
A catalogue record for this book is available from the British Library

Library of Congress Cataloging-in-Publication Data
Clayton, Mike.
  Brilliant stress management : how to manage stress in any situation / Mike Clayton. -- 1st ed.
        p. cm.
  Includes bibliographical references and index.
  ISBN 978-0-273-75054-3 (pbk. : alk. paper) 1. Stress (Psychology)
2. Stress management I. Title.
  BF575.S75C56 2011
  155.9'042--dc23
                                    2011023360

10 9 8 7 6 5 4 3 2 1
15 14 13 12 11

Typeset in 10pt Plantin by 3
Printed by Ashford Colour Press Ltd., Gosport

Contents

About the author

Mike Clayton has been stressed all of his life. He has a classic Type A personality, which compels him to do more and more; so learning how to manage his stress has always been a priority – even if making the time to do it hasn't!

Mike started his career in academic research, before moving to management consultancy to find a more pressured environment. He found it. For 12 years, he served clients in the public, voluntary and commercial sectors, working with organisations like the Ministry of Defence, Transport for London, BAA, Vodafone and General Motors, on behalf of Deloitte.

For the last nine years, Mike has focused on training and speaking. This has given him the opportunity to research what he had already started to learn, and to develop his thinking on how to present it. For the last five years, 'It ain't the stress that does the damage' has been one of Mike's most popular talks.

Having spent the first 30 years of his life wondering how anyone could live anywhere but London, Mike now lives, with his family, in a small town in Hampshire, which is less stressful by far.

Acknowledgements

I have known stress in my time, but the single most valuable thing I learned was how to meditate, in 1989; and I cannot find any record of the names of the people who taught and supported me. If you are reading this, thank you.

I would like to acknowledge all that I learned from my Aikido teachers and colleagues, and particularly Senseis David Currie and Alan Mars of the British Ki Aikido Association, and Sensei Andy Shakeshaft of the Ki Federation of Great Britain.

I also learned a lot about stress from working in a high-stress environment, so thank you to all my bosses, managers and clients, from my years at CSL Group and Deloitte – I'd best not name the ones who gave me the most to practise on!

I would like to thank Abigail Pavitt for showing me the impact of one simple action: removing my watch; and Cryss Mennaceur for giving me the opportunity to develop my thinking about stress into a successful keynote presentation, which gave this book its structure and much of its material.

Finally, one woman is most important of all: thank you, Felicity, for teaching me about happiness.

Introduction

King Solomon was King of Israel three thousand years ago. He was famed for the wealth of his cities, the magnificence of his temples and, most of all, for the wisdom of his rule. Finding it was lonely ruling a vast kingdom, Solomon wanted some way to change his mood whenever he chose. He called to his court the finest craftsmen and wisest counsellors in the land.

Make me a ring and on it engrave an inscription. Put on it words that can change my mood, whatever it is; from sorrow to joy, or from joy to sorrow.

The counsellors wrestled with the task for many months and sought the wisest sages throughout the world, until finally they had the answer. They went to the craftsman who had struck the finest ring ever made and instructed him what to engrave. At last, they presented the ring to Solomon. On the ring was engraved:

This too shall pass.

What Solomon's advisors knew was this: whatever you are going through now, this too shall pass.

Stress quiz

How stressed are you now? You might like to complete this quick quiz to find out. Rate each of these 20 statements on a scale of one to four, according to how often you feel this way, with: 0 for Never, 1 for Sometimes, 2 for Often, and 3 for Always.

1   I contain all my feelings until I want to explode.

2   I want everything now – particularly in shops.

3   I get angry and frustrated at little things.

4   Criticism and negative feedback really get to me.

5   I blame myself when things go badly.

6   Work and unwanted obligations take over my life.

7   I am too busy to enjoy my lunch breaks.

8   I don't make time to prioritise my workload.

9   The work I do is too far beyond or far below my capabilities.

10   People seem to take advantage of me.

11   I have no time for my hobbies and interests.

12   I have far too many tasks to do at work.

13   I get to work late and am late for meetings.

14   I'm in a hurry – even if there is no deadline.

15   I don't like the changes that seem to happen.

16   I don't say what I am really feeling.

17   I get angry with people who are important to me.

18   The bad things seem to outweigh the good things.

19   I struggle to cope under pressure.

20   Taking time to relax makes me feel guilty.

What is your total stress score? If it is less than 20, well done. You can put this book down now, unless you are reading it for research, to help someone else, or 'just in case'. If you scored over 40, then shut the door, turn off your phone, and read on now.

How *Brilliant Stress Management* is structured

The secret of managing stress is recognising that stress arises when we feel a lack of control in some area of our lives. *Brilliant Stress Management* will give you everything you need to start to manage your stress, from understanding what it is, to a whole heap of measures and tactics to help you regain control in specific stressful situations of work, change and conflict. It ends with tips on how to help others to control their stress. Here is a summary of each of the twelve chapters.

Chapter 1: What stress is and is not

This introductory chapter tells you about what stress is and is not. You will be able to recognise the signs of stress in yourself, and understand the basics of the physiology of stress. You will see why it isn't the stress that does the damage. Managing stress is all about regaining control.

Chapter 2: Control your physical response to stress

The first point of control is in your physical response to stress. This chapter looks at a remedial physical response to stress and also a proactive physical regime that will reduce your stress levels through: good posture, good humour, good fuel (food and drink), good rest (sleep and relaxation) and good energy (exercise).

Chapter 3: Control your environment

You will learn how simple approaches to controlling your environment can have a big effect on your stress levels. We will look at the impact of people, organisation, space, light, colour and scent.

Chapter 4: Control your time

Any guide to stress management must include the fundamentals of time management. You will learn the basics of prioritisation, planning, how to say 'no' and, perhaps most important, how to handle a sense of 'overwhelm'.

Chapter 5: Control your attitudes

We get our attitudes, values and beliefs about life from many sources, but we rarely sit down and choose them as adults. By reviewing your attitudes to a range of situations, you can reduce your stress levels by changing your response to common situations in your life.

Chapter 6: Control your mental response to stress

What goes on in your brain has a profound impact on how stressful you find a situation. This chapter looks at the ways you can control your mental response to stress, by controlling: how you visualise a situation in advance, the little voice in your head, and what you focus on when something happens.

Chapter 7: Manage stress at work

How you can recognise the signs of stress in colleagues and in your whole team. An introduction to workplace responsibilities around stress, and some of the solutions that will reduce the stress you place your colleagues and yourself under.

Chapter 8: Manage stress caused by change

Change is stressful. This chapter will help you to understand why, and will give you resources to manage your stress levels during times of change.

Chapter 9: Manage stress caused by conflict

An introduction to how you cán deal with conflicts, to help reduce the stress of your relationships in the most challenging times.

Chapter 10: Help others to manage their stress

The final chapter is designed to give you some techniques to listen and to help guide and counsel others in managing their stress levels.

Medical warning

Throughout this book, you will find contact details for national organisations with deep expertise and professionalism. If the stress you suffer from is severe, then this book can only be an introduction and you must refer yourself to an expert.

Some apparent symptoms of stress can have medical causes and need professional attention. Some effects of stress can cause medical problems. This is not a medical text and neither is the author medically qualified, so if you are in any doubt whatsoever, please contact your general practitioner straight away.

Only follow the advice in this book in so far as you are completely comfortable. It has been written with great care, but your health and your wellbeing are your responsibility.

CHAPTER 1

What stress is and is not

We all think we know what stress is and that we can easily recognise its symptoms. It seems that stress has become more common in today's society and there is a risk that familiarity will breed contempt for it. But the long-term effects of stress are worthy of far greater respect: stress can destroy lives and families.

This chapter sets out to ensure that you can recognise the signs of stress in yourself, so that you can take it seriously. It will examine the science behind stress: the way our bodies are designed to respond, and attempts to predict stress in people. This will lead us to a formal understanding of what stress is, which will be the basis for learning how to control it – and controlling stress is the basis of this book.

Signs of stress

The earliest symptoms of stress are often subtle. A bit of anxiety, feeling a little blue, getting easily flustered and angry, and tiredness are all early warnings. You may also notice changes in yourself and in your behaviour. Let's look at some of the common signs of stress.

Emotional signs of stress

As we get stressed, our levels of anxiety can cause us to respond less appropriately to unexpected and unwanted events. Do you sometimes find yourself overly defensive or aggressive – sometimes even looking for arguments? Do you feel detached from life, wanting to withdraw? Maybe your confidence has dropped noticeably and you find yourself feeling guilty or inadequate about every little failing.

Physical and mental signs of stress

One of the first features of stress is often poor or irregular sleep patterns, leaving you constantly tired (and anxious at bedtime). You also start to get every little bug going around, leading to a feeling of a constant cold with runny nose and sore throat. Other signs of diminishing health are skin problems and cold sores. Your digestion seems a little unreliable, leading to diarrhoea or constipation, and maybe you get more headaches than you used to. Back and neck pain can often follow and all of this leads to poor concentration and panic at not getting things done or not being able to cope. There are a host of other signs too, like an uncontrollable little twitch in one eye and a drop in your libido.

Important note: Some of these symptoms could also be signs of illness. If you are in any doubt, contact your general practitioner.

Behavioural signs of stress

A rush-rush busy-busy lifestyle is not just a trigger, but a symptom of stress, which leads to working longer and longer hours. This leaves you less time to relax and take care of yourself, so your appearance can start to suffer, as will your diet. More fast food, sugary or caffeine drinks, chocolate, nicotine and alcohol all indicate that you are trying to cope with stress; maybe you have lost your appetite or, paradoxically, find yourself overeating. You may also notice yourself becoming more irritable and argumentative as your patience is tried more and more. Impatience leads to a short temper, forgetfulness and more mistakes and accidents. You are becoming a danger to yourself and others.

brilliant exercise

Assess your symptoms. Count how many of each type of symptom you have on a regular or long-term basis.

Emotions

1 Anxiety

2 Tearfulness

3 Aggressiveness

4 Withdrawal

5 Guilt

6 Inadequacy

Physical symptoms

1 Dodgy tummy

2 Headaches

3 Back, neck or shoulder pain

4 Poor sleep

5 Constant illnesses

6 Loss of sex drive

Changes in your behaviour

1 Working long hours

2 Bad diet

3 Argumentative and short-tempered

4 Forgetful

5 Less attention to your appearance and self-care

6 Making mistakes

Physiology of stress

There was a time when your ancient ancestors lived in a ruthless environment, long before the *brilliant* series of books appeared. Every day a lion, or a bear, or something even bigger and uglier woke up and it knew that, if it did not catch some tasty morsel, it would go to sleep hungry. And at the same time, every morning, when your ancestors woke up, they knew that, if they did not keep out of the jaws of all those creatures, they would never go to sleep again.

The good news is that your ancestors did all survive ... at least long enough to have healthy children. The bad news is that those children – and you in your turn – have inherited a fight-or-flight response, which is poorly designed for life in the twenty-first century. Whenever your brain detects stress, it responds in just the same way as your ancestors'. Somewhere between 20 and 30 different stress hormones are released into your bloodstream and, together, they have a massive impact on you. Your natural response to stress comes from the effect of these hormones.

Your senses become more acute, your breathing becomes faster and shallower, your pulse rate shoots up, and your muscles get tense, ready to spring into action. You sweat, you become anxious, you want to run away!

And at the same time as this part of your nervous system – called your sympathetic nervous system – jumps into overload, your body shuts down the other part of your nervous system, which is responsible for immunity, repair, digestion, sleep regulation and sexual function.

So, as if it isn't bad enough that when we are stressed we tense up, we sweat and our hearts race, but we also lose our appetite, can't sleep, get spots and lose our sex drive!

Figure 1.1 illustrates the main elements of our physiological response to stress.

The amygdala detects danger and the hypothalamus signals the adrenal glands above the kidneys to secrete adrenaline (flight) and noradrenaline (fight) hormones into the bloodstream.

The pituitary gland releases adrenocorticotrophin hormone into the blood. This triggers release of a cascade of hormones, including cortisol.

Adrenaline boosts heart rate and increases breathing, wakefulness and concentration.

Adrenaline also shuts down the blood supply to the gut, turning off the digestive system, and skin to reduce possible bleeding…

… while boosting blood supply to the major muscles.

Cortisol raises blood pressure and causes the release of fats and glucose into the bloodstream, ready to fuel the muscles. It also inhibits the immune system and boosts memory formation.

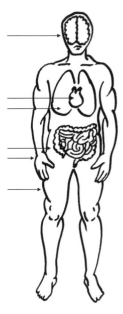

Figure 1.1 The physiology of stress

All of these changes have positive short-term effects that allow us to cope with a sudden threat, but adverse long-term effects that, if they persist, will do you the harm that we recognise as the symptoms of stress. Part of brilliant stress control and management is finding time to let the stress hormones discharge fully, before the next onslaught.

The good news for managing immediate threats

Your sympathetic nervous system jumps into overload:

- Your senses get more acute and you become more alert.
- Your breathing and heart rates increase, bringing more oxygen to your muscles.

- Your muscles get ready for action.
- You will notice increased sweating, to keep your muscles cool.
- Your blood thickens, ready to clot more easily, if you are hurt.
- Your hunger is suppressed, so you can focus on the threat at hand.

The bad news for your long-term health

Your parasympathetic nervous system shuts down:

- Your immune system is suppressed.
- Digestion stops.
- Your sleep is inhibited.
- You experience a depressed libido.
- Your heart is under increased pressure.

Type A and Type B

In the 1950s, heart specialists Dr Meyer (Mike) Friedman and Dr Ray Rosenman observed that a majority of their patients had a consistent set of personality and behaviour traits, which led them to dub such people as Type A personalities. In contrast to others (Type B personalities), they argued that Type As had an increased risk of heart disease. Their original research was first published in an academic journal in 1959 and their subsequent 1974 book, *Type A Behaviour and your Heart*, became a best-seller.

 activity

Are you a Type A or a Type B?

Score yourself on a scale of 0 to 6. Score low numbers according to how like the statements on the left you are, and high numbers if you are more like the corresponding statement on the right.

Casual and relaxed	0 1 2 3 4 5 6	Often feel on edge
Slow and deliberate	0 1 2 3 4 5 6	Always rushing
Dislike deadlines	0 1 2 3 4 5 6	Love working to deadlines
Not competitive	0 1 2 3 4 5 6	Highly competitive
Patient	0 1 2 3 4 5 6	Impatient
Many non-work interests	0 1 2 3 4 5 6	Very much work focused
Express your feelings	0 1 2 3 4 5 6	Suppress your feelings
One thing at a time	0 1 2 3 4 5 6	Lots of things at once
Ready in advance	0 1 2 3 4 5 6	Just in time
Plan and prepare	0 1 2 3 4 5 6	Just do it
Enjoy relaxing	0 1 2 3 4 5 6	Feel guilty when relaxing
Listen and consider	0 1 2 3 4 5 6	Jump to conclusions
Take things as they come	0 1 2 3 4 5 6	Measure and evaluate everything
Happy with what you have	0 1 2 3 4 5 6	Always want more
Relaxed by disagreement	0 1 2 3 4 5 6	Hostile and angry

```
◄──── Type B ────      ──── Type A ───►
   10    20    30    40    50    60    70    80    90
```

What are Types A and B?

Type A behaviours include a sense of urgency and a need to get as much done as possible. In the car park of Friedman's and Rosenman's clinic, all the visitors would typically back their cars into parking spaces to allow a quick getaway. Patients of other clinics parked more randomly. Type As are competitive, impatient and often hostile.

Friedman and Rosenman concluded that by spotting Type A behaviour they could predict heart disease.

How significant are Types A and B?

The good news is that further studies have shown that Type A behaviour, as Friedman and Rosenman defined it, is not a reliable predictor of heart disease – phew. But one aspect of it is: hostility. In numerous studies, general hostility is associated with increased mortality from heart disease and, indeed, a number of other diseases.

How this happens is not clear, and some evidence is contradictory.

For example, some experiments suggest that expressing anger heightens the link to heart disease and others suggest that suppression is more significant. What is clear is that, when we suppress our emotions, our bodies increase the physiological changes they cause.

Since provocation causes our bodies to release the fight (noradrenaline) and flight (adrenaline) hormones, suppressing our emotions can increase our hormonal response. Over a long period, this will lead to increased stress.

Type T

Adrenaline is the hormone responsible for the 'rush' of increased heart rate and oxygen flow we get when we feel under threat – whether from an unwanted source or when we seek out our thrills. However, different people feel that rush with less or more provocation. Dr David McCobb is a biologist specialising in the brain at Cornell University. He has found evidence of two different versions of a protein that is fundamental to the rate of release of adrenaline.

Anxiety is related to an increase in one form of the protein, leading to the ready release of adrenaline under low levels of threat. On the other hand, the second form of the protein dampens adrenaline release, meaning that it takes more provocation to get the same physiological response.

This provides the first hint of an explanation of why some people don't just cope well under pressure: they seek it out. Psychologist Frank Farley refers to these people as *Type T* where the T stands for Thrill. Type Ts like extreme sports and risk taking, and appear remarkably calm in situations that would rattle the rest of us.

Stress or strain?

Stress is an external stimulus. It's all of the day-to-day, week-to-week problems and difficulties we have to face; it's the angry boss, the aggressive driver, the rude shop assistant, the pressing deadline, the stupid helpdesk and the queue that never moves in the supermarket. It's the endless list of things we have to do.

We all have this in our lives, so why is it that some people let themselves get really stressed and uptight and frustrated and angry; and then make themselves really ill? At the same time, others seem to take it all in their stride; they're cool, they're relaxed, they just handle it … nothing seems to stress them.

Most of us live somewhere in the middle and our response varies from time to time. So if this is true, it can't be the external stimulus that does the damage. It must be something in us.

Some physics

I have a PhD in physics, and in physics we define terms very precisely. *Stress* is a set of forces applied to an object. Those forces cause the object to deform in some way, and that deformation is called *strain*. Taking these definitions, we can see that, in our lives, stresses are the external forces in your life. Strain is your

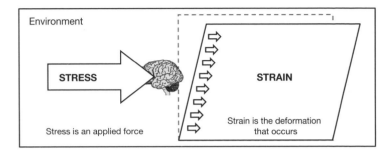

Figure 1.2 Stress and strain

body's, your emotional and your behavioural responses to the stress.

> it is not the stress that does the damage to you. It is the strain

It is not the stress that does the damage to you. It is the strain: your response. More particularly, it is the long-term effects of that strain.

Stress can be a good thing

Short-term stress is good – it can rev you up to perform well. So 'good' stress includes taking on an exciting challenge, recognising pressure to meet an important deadline, or even sensing that something is wrong and you need to seek out help and support.

brilliant example

Robert had been a stage actor for nearly 20 years when stage fright first struck him. At the time, he was playing the king in *Hamlet*. He confided in his colleague, Anne, whom he had known since drama school.

'Whenever I think about going on stage, my palms start to sweat, my heart pounds, I feel a little dizzy and a little sick, and I know I am just terrified about walking on.'

Anne recognised those symptoms; she'd had them for her whole career:

'Whenever I think about going on stage,' she said, 'I feel my heart racing, my mouth dries up and my palms start to sweat, I get that horrid feeling in my tummy, and I know I am pumped up and ready to walk on.'

Your fight-or-flight response simply means you feel threatened. How you interpret that threat — as a real danger, or pressure to perform at your best, is up to you.

A definition of stress

To avoid confusion, in *Brilliant Stress Management*, we will refer to the unwanted external pressures in your life as *stressors*, and your response to those stressors as *stress*. We will adopt the UK Health and Safety Executive's definition of stress.

brilliant definition

The adverse reaction people have to excessive pressure or other types of demand placed on them.

Health and Safety Executive (www.hse.gov.uk)

So, we feel stress when the pressures on us are too much for our ability to cope with them. Look back at the example of actors Robert and Anne: for Robert, the pressure feels too much for him, whilst, for Anne, it is just the cue she needs to give her best performance.

Long-term strain

When your body is under strain for a long time, and you do not have the opportunity to discharge the stress from time to time, you will be at risk of a wide range of serious medical problems. Chronic back pain can lead to severe damage like a prolapsed or ruptured disc, and elevated heart rate can lead to high blood pressure, cardiovascular disease, strokes and heart attack. Lowered immunity can lead to increased susceptibility to serious infections and has been implicated in increases in the malignancy of certain cancers.

Psychologically, anxiety and withdrawal can trigger underlying mental illnesses, anxiety disorders and social phobias, or depression. The implications of long-term stress on family life can also be severe: conflict, impotence or frigidity, and even breakdowns do occur.

In responding inappropriately to long-term stress, abuse of alcohol, tobacco and controlled drugs are common, as are a range of eating disorders that can lead to obesity, or malnourishment. Violent thoughts can be turned outwards, towards the people around us, or inwards, into self-destructive behaviours, self-harm, and even suicidal thoughts.

Stressors in your life

We all have stressors in our lives. The first steps to *brilliant* stress management are to recognise them and understand how much stimulation will keep you at optimum levels of arousal and productivity.

Minimum stress

It is a fallacy to believe that too much pressure is the only source of stress. Too little pressure and stimulation can, over a long period, be equally stressful. Figure 1.3 illustrates how there is an optimum level of stimulation that allows each of us to be at our best. That level will be different for you and for me. We are also well able to withstand short periods of over-load and under-load, finding the over-load exciting for a time and the under-load relaxing.

However, if the degree and the duration of over-load or under-load are too great, then each can become a stressor. Once again, your thresholds and mine will be different.

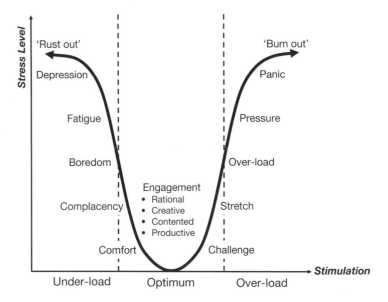

Figure 1.3 The effects of under-load and over-load on your stress levels

What are your stressors?

The three main sources of stress are major changes in our lives, relationships and work. Let's take a look at some of the typical stressors of each.

Work stressors

Any change in your workplace can be stressful, from a new role to a new boss, to a new location. But there are times when all of these can remain constant, but the pressure to perform well can increase, due to economic circumstances, customer demand, earlier problems, or even in response to a boss who is him- or herself responding to stress they are under. These are further exacerbated if you also have to cope with unreliable equipment, flawed processes, unhelpful colleagues or a frustrating daily commute. If you work unsocial hours or are frequently away from home, then these can add still further to the stress you (and your relationships) are under. Chapter 7 is devoted to managing stress at work.

Change stressors

Clearly, any form of traumatic experience or serious illness or injury is a big stressor, as is the loss of a loved one or the breakdown of an important relationship. Leaving home for the first time, loss of a job, moving home and life transitions like the birth of a child, children leaving home, and retirement are also important stressors. Chapter 8 focuses on managing stress from change.

Relationship stressors

Simply maintaining a relationship is hard work, so when that relationship faces challenges, they will be stressful. Whether at home, at work or in a social setting, conflicts can arise and, if they persist, they will take their toll. Chapter 9 examines managing stress from conflict.

brilliant exercise

How many stressors do you have?

Work stressors

1 Changes

2 Pressure to work harder

3 Poor resources (equipment, processes, materials)

4 Colleagues

5 Travel

6 Long or antisocial hours

Change stressors

1 Injury or illness

2 Traumatic experience

3 Death or illness of a loved one

4 Pregnancy or a new baby

5 Job loss or retirement

6 Moving home

Relationship stressors

1 Divorce, separation or relationship breakdown

2 Marriage or moving in with a partner

3 Major decisions and disputes

4 Sexual problems

5 Major holidays and festivals

6 Parent–child problems

The secret of managing stress: control

The importance of control

The fact that the symptoms of what we call 'stress' arise from your internal response is good news. If it is something inside ourselves, then it is also something that we can control. And if there is one single concept that sums up the source of stress and its solution, it is *control*. Stress comes from feeling that we do not have control and we solve it by regaining control – control of ourselves, control of our fear, control of our impulses and even control of our environment.

stress comes from feeling that we do not have control

In Figure 1.4, it is the things that concern you, but that you cannot control, which cause you stress. Brilliant stress management is about two things:

1 Focusing on the things that you can control, while accepting what you cannot.

2 Testing the boundaries to extend your zone of control to its fullest extent.

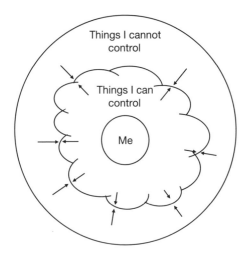

Figure 1.4 Control in your life

Choice

How you respond to stress is your choice. The one source of all your feelings of being stressed is your mind. The stress does not do the damage – rather, it is the way you respond to it that does the damage, or not.

▶ brilliant example

Think about a dried-up old tree with shallow roots and brittle twigs. If we put that tree under stress, what will happen? In a strong wind, it may blow over … or it may simply snap in two.

Now think of a mighty oak tree, with deep roots and a solid trunk. In the same wind, under the same stress, it just does not move. Its roots go deep into the solid ground and its trunk is strong and confident. Or think of a thin, supple willow. In the greatest of gales it bends and twists, moving this way and that, absorbing the stresses without leaving the place it is rooted to. Each has a different kind of strength – but each is equally strong.

The external stressors in your life are like that gale. How you respond to them is your choice.

Four failures to control

Before we look at taking control, which will fill the rest of this book, let's start by recognising the ways people find to relinquish control over their lives. Each one is a way to avoid responsibility for our own stress.

Denial

'There is no problem', 'I *am* in control', 'it's only temporary'. How often have you heard yourself deny what you know deep down: you are in trouble. But don't be too hard on yourself: denial is the first response we all have to adverse change, so these responses are totally natural. We've spent a lot of this chapter referring to your 'fight-or-flight' response, but the first reflex we all have when faced with danger is neither fight nor flight: it is *fright*. Like a hedgehog facing an articulated lorry, we want to curl up into a small ball and hope it goes away.

Splat!

Withdrawal

If you stay in your little ball and hide from the world, then, even if you accept you have a problem with stress, you will get nowhere with controlling it. Locking yourself away may feel like a positive action – stopping others from being hurt by your mood swings, perhaps. At the very best, however, it is a temporary fix, not even the start of a real solution.

Blame

Blame is for God and small children.

Louis Dega (played by Dustin Hoffman) in *Papillon*, screenplay by Dalton Trumbo and Lorenzo Semple Jr, based on the book by Henri Charrière

Another reaction that avoids your taking responsibility is to lay the blame elsewhere: on events, on equipment failures, on other people. If the source of the problem is not your fault, then you can excuse yourself the responsibility for its outcomes. This is a foolish attitude; fault and blame are the wrong concepts. It is important to understand what the stressors are, so you can deal with your response to them, and possibly deal with them directly. But all of the responsibility for yourself lies with you.

asking for help is not shirking responsibility: it is finding a way to take it

It is important to add, though, that this does *not* mean that you must go it alone. Asking for help is not shirking responsibility: it is finding a way to take it.

Distraction

If all else fails, do something else to put your stresses out of your mind. If this is part of a reasoned strategy to reduce your stress, then go ahead. If this is running away from reality, think again!

Seize control

Brilliant stress management is about how you can take control of your situation and control your stress. The first three steps are:

1 Own up to your stress.

2 Find someone to talk to.

3 Control your behavioural response to stress.

This is the sequence you should follow and is also in order of increasing challenge. When you have made good progress on each of these, you will be able to tackle a range of more powerful approaches, set out in Chapters 2 to 6. Those chapters are not in any order, and offer you choices and options. Some will be right for you, now. Others will serve well at other times or be better suited to different people in other circumstances.

1. Own up to your stress

Before you can do anything about your stress, you must be absolutely honest with yourself:

● How am I feeling?

● Which of my behaviours do I not want?

● What things are causing me stress?

● What is the range of possible consequences?

● How bad is it, on a scale of one to ten?

2. Find someone to talk to

Sharing your problem and asking for help is doing something positive. Turning to a friend, a colleague or a professional for support can help in two ways:

1 The emotional support can help you to express how you feel and release some of the emotional pressures you are feeling.

2 Another person may be able to help you find – or even offer you – practical solutions to help you regain the control you have lost.

The sooner you can access this help, the better. Ask explicitly for help, telling the other person why it is important to you, and invite them to suggest a time and a place where they will be able to give you the attention you need.

3. Control your behavioural response to stress

On pages 8–10 you learned about Type A behaviour. It may not kill you, but it isn't doing you any good. The second piece of good news is that you can modify that behaviour. Indeed, this is exactly what Meyer Friedman did, after a heart attack at the age of 55. He saw in himself a strong Type A personality and set out to change it. He died at age 90, in 2001.

Here are six strategies to reduce your Type A behaviour.

Smiling
Look for opportunities to smile – whether it is through looking for the humour in a situation or by deliberately smiling when you want to scowl.

Deliberate slowness
Force yourself to slow down. Choose the slow-moving lane on the motorway, wait patiently to cross the road, offer people a chance to step ahead of you in a queue. Look for opportunities to challenge your 'rush-rush-hurry-hurry' instinct.

Associations
The people we associate with have a huge impact on our behaviours, so spend less time with your Type A colleagues and friends and more time with Type Bs.

Planning and time management

Type A behaviour is often reactive and last-minute, so make a point of planning your time and actively managing what responsibilities you take on, and what you reject. There is much more on this in Chapter 4.

Non-competitive activities

Competitive activities can bring out the worst in Type As. So replace some of your competitive activities with other, non-competitive activities.

Reduce hostility

Reducing your levels of hostility towards the people around you will have perhaps the biggest effect on your long-term health. One way to do this is to daily make a mental list of the people you are likely to meet today and, for each one, think of one thing you particularly like, value or respect about them.

 brilliant recap

- There are a host of emotional, physical and behavioural signs of stress. Stay alert for them and, if in any doubt about their cause, contact your qualified medical practitioner.

- Stress is a natural response to a threat. In nature, our response is designed to subside with time: in our modern lives, it persists because we feel under constant, low-level threat.

- Type A behaviour can lead to stress, and hostility often leads to heart diseases − and others. You can modify these behaviours.

- Work, changes in our lives, and relationships are common stressors.

- The key to dealing with stress is to regain a sense of control in your life.

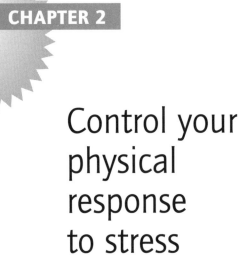

CHAPTER 2

Control your physical response to stress

The first aspect of stress that you can control is your physical response to it. Much of the damage caused by long-term exposure to stressors comes about from the poor choices we make about diet and exercise. Stress causes our muscles to tense up, affecting our relaxation and our posture, and we fail to find time for important stress-reducing activities like exercise and enjoying ourselves.

This chapter examines five points of control that you have, and how you can exercise that control to both reduce the effects of stress and also reduce the amount of stress you feel yourself under. We will look at:

- *Good posture* – the way that you use your body throughout the day can affect your wellbeing, and some simple exercises will help you to maintain good posture and relaxed muscles.

- *Good rest* – the importance of relaxing and sleeping well, and some advice on how to get a good night's sleep.

- *Good humour* – why laughter sometimes really is the best medicine, when it comes to stress.

- *Good energy* – exercise will help you build the energy that you need to fight the symptoms of a stressful life and reduce your response to stressors.

- *Good fuel* – we are, literally, what we eat. Our bodies incorporate the chemicals we put into them to build the chemicals they need to keep us healthy. Good choices about nutrition and diet make a valuable contribution to controlling stress.

The chapter ends with two sections on the use of legal drugs, and on what research tells us about healthy ageing.

An important note about this chapter:

Only carry out the exercises and advice in this chapter if you are in good health and fit. Otherwise, always consult your qualified medical practitioner first. If in doubt, check it out.

Good posture

Your nervous system does not just connect your brain to your body – it also connects your body back to your brain. Changing your physiology sends powerful signals to your brain to release different hormones that change the way you feel. How we stand, sit and use our bodies can have a profound effect on our mood.

As you feel your muscles start to tense up, make a conscious decision to relax them. When you do this, you will get the double benefit.

Benefit 1: Reduced harm

Releasing the tension will reduce the harm that it does to your musculoskeletal system (causing aching around the neck, shoulders, back and hips, which can be followed by more serious harm). It will also reduce pressure on your arteries that restricts blood flow to your brain (causing reduced concentration and 'tension headaches').

Benefit 2: Increased sense of wellbeing

Your body, nervous system and brain form a positive feedback loop: when your brain detects tension it thinks 'There's something wrong: tense up!' This makes the tension worse ... and so on. If your brain gets signals telling it your body is relaxing, it will think 'Everything's okay now: relax!'

Posture and movement

The first step to taking control of your posture is to become aware of the way your body feels when you stand, sit or move. Does it feel completely relaxed and free, or are you aware of any points of tension or tightness where you are holding yourself stiffly or your movement is not as fluid as you would like?

Progressive relaxation

For most of us, this bodily awareness does not come naturally; it takes practice. So start off, when you have finished this paragraph, by putting this book down and taking an inventory of your body. Start with your feet and work your way up. As you notice a little tension in a muscle, release it. Don't let yourself go all floppy and limp, but allow your different muscles to work together and balance one another. Work your way up your legs, paying attention to the joints at your ankles, knees, then hips. Now work through your trunk and chest to your shoulders, which often carry a lot of tension. Notice your breathing, before you work down your arms, relaxing your shoulders, elbow and wrists, ending up with a soft feeling in your hands and fingers. Now return to your neck. Let it relax and straighten, and feel your head perfectly balanced. Relax your facial muscles, allowing your expression to soften, your eyes to defocus a little, and your tongue to relax in your mouth.

Try it now.

Good posture

Having a good posture is not only good for your health and fitness; it also leads to a greater 'presence' that conveys confidence and authority to the people around you. Our bodies are designed to adopt a natural posture that is well balanced, but the muscle tensions that frequently accompany stress pull our joints this way and that, upsetting the balance and leading to a wide range of poor postures. These in turn give rise to all sorts of long-term problems and even disabilities.

If you have any concerns that your posture is asymmetric, twisted or bent in a direction that it should not be, or if you have any serious or chronic muscle or joint pain, you must see a suitably qualified medical practitioner. These things can usually be put right quickly and painlessly if treated early but, if left, can take far longer to resolve. Often, your general practitioner will refer you to an osteopath or a chiropractor, and you may choose, if you are confident that your discomfort is joint or muscle related, to visit an osteopath or chiropractor without consulting a GP. Do ensure that whoever you select is fully registered by the appropriate professional body. If you can get a personal recommendation from somebody you know, all the better.

Sitting and standing

Standing up

Perhaps the most natural posture for us is standing up. When you do so, good posture should come naturally to you, but to help you find it, here are a few tips. First, your feet should be flat on the floor, about shoulder width apart. You will notice that they are not naturally parallel, but a little splayed outwards. Notice any tension in your ankles, calves and knees, and adjust the amount of splay, until you are at your most comfortable. You should also notice an equal weight on each foot and, as you do so, become aware of how each foot is like a tripod, with your weight shared between three points: your heel and two pads behind your big toe and your little toe. The pads of your toes also bear weight, but when you are still and balanced, they should only do so minimally. They principally help balance you as you move.

Further up your body, notice your hips. These should be aligned to face forward, with weight evenly carried by each. Now release your tummy muscles and get a sense of relaxation lengthening your back and widening your shoulders and chest. Imagine that there is a puppet string attached to the very top of your head. Imagine that this string is being pulled upwards, straightening your neck gently and allowing your head to sit easily on your neck. Hang your arms comfortably by your sides, with your hands and fingers relaxed – neither in a fist, nor overly straightened.

Sitting down

Many of us like to just flop into a chair. It feels relaxing and, when we are fully relaxed, it will do us little harm. When you are carrying a bundle of muscle tensions, however, this can emphasise the imbalances and increase the damage that they create. Good posture when sitting down is as important as your standing posture and there are a few tips to getting it right.

The first tip is to select a chair of the right height for your body, or either pad the seat (if it is too low) or use a foot rest or a couple of books to support your feet (if it is too high). You should find that, with your thighs level on your chair and your knees bent at right angles, your feet rest easily on the floor with no tension.

Rest your weight evenly on the two 'sitting bones' (your ischia) inside each buttock and allow your ankles and knees to relax. Once again, imagine that puppet string gently guiding your head upwards, allowing your back and neck to lengthen along the direction of your spine.

The Alexander Technique

The two sets of tips above, standing up and sitting down, are based on the Alexander Technique. This is a set of techniques that you can learn, and which help practitioners to understand how we use our bodies and gently improve our posture. If you want to learn how to relax your body and improve your posture, or develop more even breathing to improve your speaking, singing or music playing, then this is an excellent discipline to pursue, and you will find Alexander teachers in most towns.

The importance of movement in posture

Moving freely and easily will help keep your posture good and strong, and also improve your confidence and your mood. One simple exercise can have a rapid and surprisingly profound effect on how you feel when under mild levels of stress. You can use it at any time, to prepare for a meeting, relax before an outing, or simply to cheer yourself up after a tough day. If you are concerned about what people may think, then do it in private.

brilliant exercise

Stand up, with your feet about shoulder width apart and make yourself comfortable. Let your puppet string pull you up into a comfortable posture. Now, gently move your head to look upwards, without overstretching. Finally, bring a smile to your face – it may help you to imagine a warm sun shining down on you, so that your eyes softly close. Relax in that posture for up to a minute. You will be surprised how much of a sense of wellbeing this can bring about.

Jiggle and shake

The next exercise is a lot more dynamic and will give you a sense of energy and relaxation. It is taken from Ki Aikido, a gentle martial art, well suited to relaxing and exercising at any level. Practitioners range from young and fit people practising with astonishing energy to elderly and disabled people, practising at a level that suits their abilities.

brilliant exercise

Stand up, feet about shoulder width apart, firmly on the floor and make yourself comfortable. Allow your puppet string to draw you up into a good posture, with your arms comfortably by your sides.

Now let your fingers wiggle and, as they do, let your wrists start to shake. Let the shaking increase to include your whole arms. Then let your shoulders move too and, eventually, allow your whole body to rise up and down, on the balls of your feet.

Now, progressively reverse this. Take all your weight on your feet and then slow the shaking in your trunk, then your shoulders, gradually still your arms, and then your wrists and, finally, let your fingers come to rest.

You should notice a little tingling in the tips of your fingers. That is the sensation of oxygenated blood flowing. If it's flowing in your fingers, then it is also flowing into your head and giving your brain a good boost of oxygen.

Good rest

Rest and relaxation are an essential part of dealing effectively with stress. As we become more stressed we find it harder to relax and sleep well. And, as we get less sleep, our ability to put events into perspective

> rest and relaxation are an essential part of dealing effectively with stress

and cope with stressors diminishes. Rest and stress are part of a feedback loop, so take control and move from a vicious cycle into a virtuous cycle of good rest leading to resourceful attitudes, bringing about effective actions, that allow you to relax properly and sleep well.

Relaxing

Relaxation triggers a physiological response that is the opposite to the stress response. Now your sympathetic nervous system will reduce its activity, slowing your breathing and heart rates, while your parasympathetic nervous system takes control, re-activating your immune response, your digestive system and your natural sleep cycles. Your sex drive will surely follow.

If only you could then boost your relaxation and create a powerful sense of wellbeing. Perhaps incredibly powerful drugs might help. Drugs that are legal and completely safe to use would be ideal – and better still, free.

The drugs we are talking about are a group of natural brain chemicals called endorphins, which are responsible, wholly or in part, for senses of elation, relaxation, and pain relief. Our hypothalamus and pituitary glands (which also play a big part in our fight-or-flight response – see Chapter 1) produce them naturally at times when we exercise hard, feel love or excitement, eat spicy food, and have an orgasm.

You can also fool your brain into releasing endorphins by allowing yourself to think about a pleasurable memory in great detail. Take about 10 minutes to close your eyes and wallow in that memory, seeing the scenes you saw, hearing the sounds, smelling the smells and feeling the textures and temperature. Make it as real as you can and feel free to amplify how good it was in your memory. You can use this technique to conjure up a sense of calm, happiness, joy or anything else. Build a library of recollections or even fantasies that you can call on when you need them.

The perfect relaxing posture

We met the Alexander Technique earlier in this chapter, with some tips for standing up and sitting down. To relax completely, try lying down the Alexander way.

brilliant exercise

The Alexander semi-supine posture

Find a comfortable place on a firm floor – ideally on a carpet or exercise mat. You will need a couple of books to rest your head – approximately 5 cm thick, but take time to find the right height for you.

Lie with your bottom, back and shoulders on the floor and your head resting on your books. If you feel pressure on your chin or throat, try a smaller pile of books and, if you feel your head tilted back, try more. Bend your legs and bring your feet up, just in front of your bottom, about shoulder width apart, with your feet flat on the floor and your knees pointing upwards. Rest your hands gently on your tummy or flat on the floor beside you. Breathe steadily from deep down.

Try resting in this posture for 10 to 20 minutes – maybe combining it with a gentle meditation. Imagining yourself to be made of chocolate on a warm day works well. As you do this, feel your body melting and spreading over the floor. This will encourage your muscles to relax and your joints to lengthen and widen.

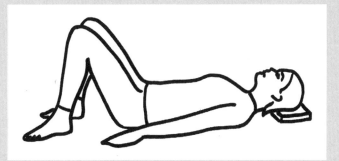

Figure 2.1 The Alexander semi-supine posture

Other routes to deep relaxation

Mankind has found a host of ways you can relax deeply, which in itself indicates how important it is to us. Here are some brilliant options. Some of them will not be for you, and may seem far out or ineffective. What matters is that you can find one or two that do work for you.

- Aromatherapy
- Body massage
- Indian head massage
- Reiki healing
- Reflexology
- Listening to music
- Performing music
- Reading
- Taking a bath
- Sitting contemplating the world
- Daydreaming
- Taking a nap
- Watching a movie
- Listening to the radio

Meditating

Meditation has a long and glorious history, with modern science only now starting to figure out why it is so valuable to us. A *New Scientist* review article published in January 2011 identified 17 benefits that have been measured in scientific studies, in the areas of behaviour, thinking, emotions and health. Of particular interest to you in controlling your stress are: reducing anxiety, combating stress, reducing emotional reactivity, helping with eating disorders, reducing depression and sustaining concentration.

brilliant exercise

Meditation

Find a comfortable upright chair somewhere where you will not be disturbed, and sit down in a good posture. Place your hands in your lap, left hand on top of right (unless you are left-handed). Gently close your eyes.

As you relax, you will start to gently focus your attention on one thing. Some people prefer a word, or mantra. In traditional Indian techniques, this may be a Sanskrit word, but you can choose any word or phrase, although something abstract will work best. You could focus on an image and, again, something abstract like a simple shape will work well. Another common approach is to focus on your breathing and, in Ki meditation, practitioners focus on a point in the centre of their abdomen, called the Hara in Japanese, Dantian in Chinese and known as your 'one-point' in English.

So, focus on the object of your meditation; I will use the word 'calm' in this example, and allow yourself to repeat it whenever it comes into your mind. Your thoughts will stray: that's natural. As soon as you notice that you are no longer focused on the word 'calm', then let go of the unwanted thoughts and bring your mind back to 'calm'. As you sit, your mind will gently settle. The unwanted thoughts will return, but simply push them gently away and return to 'calm'.

When you start, 10 minutes will seem like a long time. But gradually build up your practice to 20 minutes to get the full benefit. Meditation works best when it is regular, every day at the same time. To get the most from it, 20 minutes in the morning and then again in the evening will truly relax you and sharpen your ability to concentrate.

One thing that new meditators often find is that their body takes the opportunity, while relaxed, to get the sleep it needs. If this happens to you, do not worry; your body knows best. However, once you establish a routine, it is best to avoid times when you are over-sleepy or, indeed, overstimulated. In the morning, try meditating after you have got up and had a shower, but before you eat breakfast. When you get home from work in the evening, take some time to unwind, and then meditate before your evening meal, and before you drink any alcohol. These aren't rules, but they will help you get the best from your meditation.

Breathing

Why do smokers smoke when they are stressed? It is not just the effect of nicotine (which we will examine later); when they smoke, they breathe deeply – which their body associates with relaxation – and so they relax. So when you feel stress, make a conscious effort to breathe deeply. Stand or sit upright and take a deep breath in through your nose and exhale through your mouth. Five or six deep breaths like this can really calm you.

If you want to energise yourself, you need to get as much oxygen into your bloodstream as you can. Start with the longest out-breath that you can sustain, through your mouth. When you can go no longer, stop, pause and then expel a little more air with a 'ha' sound. Now take a deep breath in and hold it for a second or two. Then repeat the out-breath process. Now take two or three deep in-breaths through your nose, followed by out-breaths through your mouth. Finish with a deep slow in-breath. What you have done is replaced as much as possible of the stale air in your lungs. Normal out-breaths only clear half to two-thirds of the air in your lungs, so this process will replace much more of that air with new oxygen-rich air. Needless to say, the best place to do this is outside.

Sleeping

Nothing is quite so important for keeping a realistic perspective on your stressors as regular and refreshing sleep. So give sleep a high priority in your life.

The most important step if you are having trouble sleeping is to get yourself a sleep ritual that involves a regular time to go to bed and get up. Do relaxing things for at least an hour before you are ready to go to sleep, like taking a bath or listening to music. Create a regular ritual that tells your body it is getting towards time to turn off for the night. Avoid stimulants like nicotine, caffeine and alcohol for the last few hours of the day and try to finish eating at least two hours before bedtime – these all have a disruptive effect on your sleep. But do not go to bed feeling hungry. If you need to snack, avoid sugary foods and go for something like toast or cereal with milk.

Make sure your bedroom is relaxing, well ventilated and not too warm, and invest in the best mattress and pillows you can afford. Remember, you spend around one-third of your life in bed – far more than in your car or on your sofa, or watching your television.

If you are not feeling sleepy, read a book for 20 to 30 minutes, rather than lying awake, wishing you were asleep. If this is a regular problem, then get more exercise in the early evening, finishing around two hours before bedtime. The only strenuous activity that promotes sleep immediately is sex.

Pets and relaxation

Pet ownership seems to be a great way to relieve some of the symptoms of stress. As well as the healthy aspects of exercising a dog, or the way responsibility for an animal can take your mind off your own troubles, research evidence suggests that caring for a dog can reduce blood pressure and one of the most interesting reasons is that walking a dog creates social interactions where passers-by smile at the owner and even stop and chat.

Cat ownership seems to have less effect, although there is little doubt that stroking a friendly cat does produce short-term relaxation. It does, however, require a lot less commitment and may fit better with many people's lifestyles.

Good humour

The nerves connecting your brain to your mouth work in both directions. When you smile, it signals your brain that all is well and triggers the release of 'happy hormones'. Laughter is one of the greatest cures for feelings of stress and maybe is the best medicine. Make time for fun and laughter in your life.

make time for fun and laughter in your life

The average adult laughs 15 times a day, while the average four-year-old laughs 400 times.

The source of this quote is numerous websites, none of which offers any definitive evidence. But it's a great quote and, if we ignore the problem of the word average, seems to accord with experience. My toddler seems to laugh hundreds of times a day – I rarely do!

How many times have you ever thought: 'One day I'll have a good laugh about this'? Well, why not laugh about it now? Laughter is one of the most powerful ways to increase your sense of wellbeing and stimulate your parasympathetic nervous system (the healing part).

The Felicity factor

LeeAnn Harker and Dacher Keltner, at the University of California, Berkeley, studied a college yearbook, looking at the faces of every woman and identifying those that had genuine smiles. They controlled their study for factors like physical attractiveness and found that observers rated women displaying more positive emotion as having more attractive personalities. Most significantly for us, these positive emotional expressions predicted good outcomes in marriage and in personal wellbeing up to 30 years later.

This is one study among many suggesting that happy people tend to have happy lives: what I call the 'Felicity factor'. Felicity means 'happiness' or 'a cause of happiness'. It is also the name of my wife.

Finding the funny

So, assuming you aren't smiling enough in your life, where can you find the funny?

- Make time to see funny films.
- Buy your favourite TV comedy shows on DVD.
- Go to comedy clubs.
- Share a joke with friends.
- Read a funny book or cartoon strips like *Calvin and Hobbes*, *The Far Side*, *Dilbert* …
- Look for funny clips on internet video sites.

Good energy

Increased regular exercise reduces your need for sleep and generates the hormones that activate your parasympathetic (repair and maintenance) nervous system. If you don't sleep well, or enough, then building regular exercise into your routine will help. It will also have a great effect on your mood and your energy levels during the day. It is no coincidence that the busiest people take rigorous steps to protect regular exercise time. Just 20 minutes in the gym or taking a brisk walk in the fresh air will help to get your mind and body balanced.

Regular exercise does not simply mean sporting activities; your range of options is enormous. You could also try walking, jogging, gardening or dance. For more gentle exercise, you might think of tai chi, yoga or Pilates. A lot of the benefits for stress reduction can come from the social aspects of your exercise, as well as the fitness, weight control and sleep benefits.

brilliant list

Low-impact exercise

- Walking, swimming or dance
- Washing a car, vacuum cleaning or decorating
- Gardening, sweeping leaves or mowing the lawn
- Yoga, Pilates or Alexander Technique
- Chi Gung, tai chi or Ki Aikido

Whatever form of exercise you choose, pick ones that you enjoy, and start gently. The biggest risk from any exercise is starting with a burst of enthusiasm and overdoing it. This is especially so if you are either starting again after a long break, or are taking up something new and you have not yet built up the skills and experience to do it safely. If you are in any way ill, overweight, injured or disabled, get advice from your medical practitioner before taking on something new.

Good fuel

You are what you eat and drink. If you know that your diet is not what you want it to be, you won't change it until you start to recognise the link between what goes into your body and the person you are.

Your choice of what you consume will have a huge and rapid effect on your mood and your response to stress. Why do nicotine, caffeine, excess sugar and fats, and various drugs have such a massive impact on our bodies? It's because they contain powerful active chemicals. In most cases, it is this high biological activity that renders them toxic when used to excess.

Food

Dietary choices are intimately tied up with all aspects of your health, and only experts can truly hope to keep up with the constant stream of research showing heart benefits of this food and cancer risks from that. *Brilliant Stress Management* cannot give you the information you need to fine-tune your diet, but balance and moderation will always be a good starting point, as will the use of fresh, seasonal foods, with the minimum of pre-processing. Keeping your salt, saturated fat and sugar intakes to moderate levels is extremely important, and ensuring you eat good quantities of a variety of fresh fruits and vegetables will keep you feeling good.

Perhaps as important as what you eat is how you eat. Make time for your meals. Making meals a social activity and participating in their preparation will slow you down and

> perhaps as important as what you eat is how you eat

chill you out. Eating a meal at a relaxed pace and enjoying good company will help put your body in the ideal state to digest your food well.

Stress-healthy foods

Here is a list of food for which there is some evidence of stress reduction or helping your body stay healthy at times of stress.

- Fresh fruit
- Fresh vegetables – especially leafy green vegetables like cabbage, spinach and broccoli; carrots; tomatoes; onions and garlic; peas; capsicums (peppers)
- Oily fish
- Pulses and beans
- Dried fruit – but avoid sulphur-treated fruits
- Nuts and seeds
- Fruit and nut bars based on oats (not on chocolate, sorry!)
- Eggs
- Soya products like tofu
- Herb teas and infusions

Water

Your brain is like a grape – or a raisin. Very slight shortages of water – well below the level that triggers fatigue or headaches – cause your brain to shrink and wrinkle up. Not by much, but it is enough to diminish its effectiveness. Keep drinking fresh water (British tap water is very good quality) to stay at your best. Typically, you should aim for a cup an hour – more in hot weather or dry, air-conditioned environments.

Another reason to drink plenty of water is that your brain can often confuse thirst for hunger, triggering you to seek more food than you need. So, even if you don't feel thirsty, make a glass of water your first priority when you feel peckish between meals, have a headache or feel fuzzy-headed, or in any way lethargic.

A word or two about drugs – the legal ones

Most of us would like to think that we can control our stress levels without the benefit of drugs like sleeping pills, tranquillisers, anti-depressants or illegal narcotics. But how many of us are truly drug-free? Three legal drugs are widely used, yet each can do us significant harm when abused:

Caffeine
The least harmful of the three, caffeine can, nonetheless, exacerbate the problems you face when you are stressed.

Nicotine
The harm from nicotine is well documented and its use in the Western world is declining. Yet many turn to nicotine at times of stress, and smokers typically increase their intake.

Alcohol
Alcohol's potential for harm is huge, from addiction to alcohol-induced accidents. Yet it can also be used safely and, in small doses, can help alleviate some of the symptoms of stress and help promote relaxation and laughter.

We will examine these legal drugs one at a time.

Caffeine

Caffeine is a stimulant with similar physiological effects to adrenaline and, in small quantities, will do you no harm: your liver can deal with it and clear it from your system. But make no mistake: large doses of caffeine are toxic.

Too much caffeine can cause heart palpitations and it is also a diuretic, causing your kidneys to excrete more water than normal, placing you at risk of dehydration. It reduces calcium levels in your body, affecting bone growth and maintenance and, in pregnant women, high doses are implicated in low-birthweight babies.

How much caffeine is too much?

Caffeine is toxic in doses of over 300 milligrams (300 mg). This is equivalent to three mugs of instant coffee or two of brewed coffee, six cups of tea or four mugs of strong tea, eight cans of cola or four of high-caffeine 'energy' drinks. The most startling effect is how long it takes your body to clear caffeine. After around five hours, half of what you drank will still be in your system, keeping you buzzing.

While one cup from time to time can enhance your cognitive performance and memory, when you drink too much for a period of time you will be less able to concentrate, make more mistakes and find the quality of your sleep is impaired. If you recognise these symptoms, it is time to detox: stop drinking caffeine. You will probably get a severe withdrawal headache around 24 hours after your last drink, but the next day you will feel much better. Replace the caffeine with herb or fruit teas, or decaffeinated products, and drink caffeine-containing drinks now and then, as a treat.

Nicotine

Why do smokers smoke when they are stressed? Because when they do, they breathe deeply – which their body associates with relaxation and so they relax. So, when you feel stress, make a conscious effort to breathe deeply. In fact, nicotine itself is a stressor – it activates your sympathetic (fight and flight) nervous system, increasing your breathing rate, heart rate and blood pressure.

The US Center for Disease Control (CDC) estimates that, for every minute you smoke, your life expectancy drops by one minute. So for a typical 20 cigarettes a day, that could be more than 2 hours. That's a month of your life, for every year of smoking. This effect gets greater as you age, so a lifelong smoker can easily lose a decade of living. But you will look older when you die.

You will find lots of advice for giving up smoking, and the impact of doing so is pretty quick. Within 24 hours, your blood oxygen (good) level comes back up to normal and your blood carbon monoxide (bad) level drops back to near zero. Your lungs have started to clear the soot, ash and old mucus, your clean clothes smell fresh, and you have saved over £6. A month later, you are £200 better off, have no nicotine in your body, you can breathe better, and food tastes and smells wonderful – as will your house, if you have cleaned and aired it. Most important, your blood circulation is starting to improve already.

After a year, your breathing is noticeably better and you have reduced the risk of a heart attack to half that of a smoker. Think what you can do with the £2,500 you have saved. Ten years later you can buy a new car and enjoy it, knowing that your chances of getting lung cancer have reduced by 50 per cent.

Alcohol

One or two drinks, within safe limits, when you don't need to think carefully or operate machinery, are a good way to relax. But a little social drinking is the tip of a big iceberg for some.

Who would really sign up for memory loss, poor judgement, dehydration, headaches and dizziness? And these are just the short-term effects. Long-term overuse of alcohol can increase your susceptibility to heart disease, strokes, cancers (mouth, throat, breast, liver and colon), liver and pancreatic diseases, stomach problems, infertility and impotence, and osteoporosis (brittle bones). And these are completely separate from the social and emotional effects of alcohol abuse.

From time to time, medically recommended safe limits are revised. Keep reviewing these and make sensible choices. Avoid binge-drinking and keep your average consumption within safe limits. Don't go more than a few days without taking a day or two off completely, to give your liver some time to recover.

Healthy ageing

In his book *Aging Well* George Vaillant describes seven factors that promote successful physical and emotional ageing: lack of tobacco and alcohol abuse, an adaptive coping style, maintaining healthy weight, exercise, a sustained loving relationship, and years of education. Surprisingly, his research found no evidence that stress levels are a relevant factor. But look more closely and in the list you will see 'an adaptive coping style'. People who can handle stress well do indeed have an advantage.

Almeda County Study

The biggest survey of how life outcomes link to behaviour is known as the Almeda County Study, in which Dr Nedra Belloc and Dr Lester Breslow studied the lives of 7,000 people. Their results were very similar to George Vaillant's. Could it be that, together, these studies give a good prescription for controlling your physical response to stress?

Table 2.1 Belloc & Breslow's seven health factors for longevity

1 Sleep 7 to 8 hours per day

2 No eating between meals

3 Eat breakfast regularly

4 Maintain proper weight

5 Regular exercise

6 Moderate or no use of alcohol

7 No smoking

↗ brilliant resources

- If you have alcohol-related problems, Alcoholics Anonymous are a good source of help: **www.alcoholics-anonymous.org.uk**

- The Alexander Technique is unregulated in the UK. However, The Society of Teachers of The Alexander Technique (**www.stat.org.uk**) is prominent.

- Chiropractors in the UK are regulated by The General Chiropractic Council: **www.gcc-uk.org**

- To learn about Ki Aikido in the UK, contact the Ki Federation of Great Britain: **www.kifederationofgreatbritain.co.uk**

- To give up smoking in the UK, start with the NHS SmokeFree website: **www.smokefree.nhs.uk**

- Osteopaths in the UK are regulated by The General Osteopathic Council: **www.osteopathy.org.uk**

brilliant recap

- If you improve your posture, you can reduce both the feelings of stress and the damage and pain that tensed-up muscles can cause your body.

- Relaxation and sleep are vital to controlling your stress. Use techniques like meditation, and prioritise sleep, to ensure you are well rested and have a clear perspective on your situation.

- Exploit the 'Felicity factor' – happier people have better lives.

- Exercise is important to build up strength, stamina and suppleness, and reinforce your reserves against stress – it also helps your sleeping. If you aren't keen on sport, there are plenty of alternatives.

- You are what you eat, so make careful choices about what you put into your body.

- Healthy ageing is not a matter of chance or accident; you can stack the odds in your favour, with the right behaviours.

CHAPTER 3

Control your environment

Grant me the serenity to accept the things I cannot change;
The courage to change the things I can.

'The Serenity Prayer' by Reinhold Niebuhr

I n Figure 1.4, we saw the importance of a focus on the things
we can control. For example, you can sometimes completely
avoid stressful situations: you can travel the congested section
of the M25, M42, M62 or your nearest equivalent between 7.30
and 9.00 a.m., and get caught in the inevitable delays caused by
hundreds of other people doing the same. Or you can get up a
little earlier, breeze through at 7.00 a.m., and get a coffee and
sandwich at a café near your destination, and either relax or get
some useful work or reading done.

Richard Logan, at the University of Wisconsin, studied people
who had survived extremely adverse circumstances, to find out
what they had in common. One feature that was particularly
prevalent was the fact that each of them had a belief that they
were responsible for their future, despite situations that many of
us would see as beyond their control, like harsh natural environments or concentration camps.

The lesson from this is clear: there is always something you can
do to affect your situation. When you do take action, you will
feel a sense of control that will lift some of the feelings of stress.

This chapter is about how to take control of your environment: not a polar wilderness or the worst of mankind's horrors, but the everyday environment that most *Brilliant Stress Management* readers will enjoy.

We will first see a process for taking control and then examine four aspects of your environment that you can control:

1 Your social connections.

2 How you organise yourself.

3 Your living and work space.

4 Your sensory environment.

We will close the chapter by returning to the need to take action and, if that proves impossible, the importance of looking for escape routes that will take you out of your stressful environment.

Process

The process for taking control of your environment is simple – although carrying it out will not always be easy. There are four steps.

1 Believe in your power to control your life.

2 Commit to controlling your life.

3 Act on your decision.

4 Be persistent.

Let's look at these steps one at a time.

Believe

The hardest part is the first part; after this, the rest is easy. In the face of stress and adversity, you must believe in your power to control your life. This is what characterised the people that Richard Logan studied.

When you feel uncomfortable, it is a sign that something is wrong. Deep inside you, you feel that things must change. Look around at your environment and see the things that you must change. Listen to what your heart tells you about the things that you need to change.

You can get control when you make choices, so start to recognise that not only must things change, but that *you* must change them. To be in control means not waiting for events to change, or for somebody else to rescue you, which are forms of helplessness, but fundamentally to believe that *'if it is to be: it is up to me'*.

Believe that you can make choices that will control your environment. Learn to prioritise, learn to say no, learn to manage your time, learn to arrange your life in ways that suit you. Change your physical environment so that it helps you to relax, or to get things done, or to share your burden.

> learn to prioritise, learn to say no, learn to manage your time

A lot of people say they get stuck. They say they have tried – and not succeeded. Well, if you have tried, then you have made a start, but there is an old saying:

'If at first you don't succeed …'

One very simple yet powerful way to take control of your environment is to look at the space you inhabit – your office, your workstation and your home. What can you do to make it more relaxing, more efficient or more inviting? Make a great start by removing clutter and rubbish. Now think about how you could personalise it in a way that suits you and yet still meets the constraints of your organisation at work, or your family at home.

Commit

We feel under stress when we feel we have no control over what's going on around us. Believing you can take control is a start; the next step is to commit to controlling your life. The word 'decision' comes from the Latin, meaning 'to cut off from', so decisions can be scary because they reduce our options. But when you make a decision, it is also very liberating. You are cutting yourself off from a powerless state and have really started to take control.

Make a 100 per cent commitment now
Find one change that you commit to making that will exert your control over an aspect of your external environment within the next 24 hours. Make it real: find a pen or pencil and a piece of paper (the margin of this book will do) and write it down. I will wait.

Act

'*Without action, there is no change.*'

If you have written down a commitment, and if you are a person of integrity (or you would like to be from now on), you might also write down: '*What I commit to, I do.*'

Having made a commitment, the third step is to act on your decision. To feel in control, any positive action will do, so if you feel daunted by the task, feel free to start small: take one baby-step towards making the change you committed to. Another great way to spur action is to put together a simple plan, so you know what the first step is, and you can see clearly how it leads to the next and the next, and eventually to a real change. Once you take your first physical action, you will feel a huge sense of control.

Persist

So there is only one thing more you need to do: be persistent.

Remember that old saying:

'*If at first you don't succeed ...*'

Most people would complete it with the words *'try, try again'*. But that is foolish. What makes you think that, when you do what you did before, you will not get what you got before? A far more resourceful approach, and the one to remember, is:

'If at first you don't succeed, try something else.'

And if that doesn't succeed, try something else again... In response to someone who says *'I tried everything,'* my response would be: *'Really, everything?'* As soon as you believe you cannot make a change, you are back to helplessness.

If what you are doing is working, acknowledge your success, pat yourself on the back, and do more. If it is not working, do something different. Have the courage to change the things you can – and you always can. There are always changes you can make.

Social connections

One of the biggest stress factors can be not having people around us who care about us and support us. Making, protecting and using relationships with other people is a fundamental part of coping and thriving in stressful situations.

Establish healthy relationships

In the workplace, having a social network so that you can access informal support from colleagues will give you a quick outlet to minor frustrations before they become major stressors. Research in the UK Civil Service showed that staff who had social connections with colleagues felt less stressed, less anxious and suffered less absence due to psychiatric illness.

So, chats at the coffee machine, sharing a trip to the shops at lunchtime, and joining workmates for a drink after work are all good investments in your wellbeing – as well as pleasures.

Protect valuable relationships

Don't overdo the chat

If you find colleagues are wasting too much of your time in gossiping at the water fountain, it's time to politely return to work. The danger is that the gossip itself will become stressful, as your desire to be sociable conflicts with your need to meet your responsibilities at work. And if you find your work falling behind, there will be a second stressor. So a little honesty: *'I really do need to get back to my work now'* can prevent the relationship going sour, as you start to resent its intrusion on your responsibilities.

Don't take advantage

When we are under stress, we often take advantage of the generosity of the people who love us. This can mean treating them inconsiderately. But because they care for us, they will accept it as a product of our stress and be prepared to help where they can, and wait it out.

But there is only so much misuse a person can take, before their love for you starts to go sour. So it is vital, even in times of stress, to be mindful of the way you treat the people you value most in your life. It is because you sometimes can treat them badly that you must find a way to put them first.

Use relationships to help you de-stress

Releasing stress doesn't get much simpler than talking. Sadly, many of us do not find it easy, so it is essential that you find someone whom you feel you can trust, totally. Whilst some people's unwillingness to help you may be shocking, you will be surprised how many people will want to help, and will be keen to do so in a wholly supportive and non-judgemental way. So, consider each of the people around you; the 'right' person for you to choose may not be who you expect.

If you are under a lot of stress, listening is not the only thing that other people can do for you. Letting you take time to scream, rant or cry will help defuse your emotions, so that you can move into a more rational state of mind.

brilliant tip

If you really do not have someone, then finding a private space to express yourself, and writing down your feelings and frustrations are the next best thing.

Get organised

Being organised may seem like a small step that will have little effect on your stress levels, but don't underestimate it. It will be when you are at your most stressed that the inability to find that essential component or letter or tool will seem like an iceberg heading towards the bow of your ship.

Also, starting to get organised is easy, so it is an ideal way to start to seize control. The danger is that, in a time of pressure, organising yourself could become a displacement activity that does nothing more than distract you from your stress. So, follow these three simple rules for organising yourself or your work when you are feeling under stress.

Rule 1: Tidy frenzy

You don't have much time, so set yourself a strict time limit, like four minutes, to tidy your space and clear it of clutter. If you can, a good way to do this is to play a piece of fast-rhythm music that lasts three to five minutes and do as much as you can before it ends. You will be amazed at how much tidying and organising you can do under this constraint, and how good you will feel when it is done.

Rule 2: Backlog file

Organising takes time and there are lots of systems available (see, for example, Chapter 3 of *Brilliant Time Management*), but to make a lot of progress quickly you need to focus hard. Work on only what needs to be organised for you to make progress on the things that are stressing you. Put everything else into a backlog file, ready to be organised when the pressure is off, but safely stored so it is not lost.

Rule 3: Little bits

Keeping on top of your organisation can be satisfying, but don't make a big thing of it, or it will become a stressor itself. So, when the opportunity presents itself, just do one bit of organising and then go back to what you were doing. If you need to leave a workshop and will be going past the storage racks, pick up one or two things from your bench to put away. When you need to go to the filing cupboard, take a couple of papers from your desk that need to be filed. When you are putting away the pots and pans, take a moment to sort out a part of the jumble in the cupboard. Every time you do a little bit, think to yourself *'Good, that's progress'* and then move on. Now your brain will feel more in control.

Your space

It seems that the more you express yourself in your surroundings, the more relaxed you will become; so, every day do something to make your environment nicer for yourself. It does not matter how small. You might want to tidy up, pick a bunch of flowers, display a new photo or postcard, replace your old coffee or tea mug, use a nice notebook and pen, or change the desktop and colour settings on your computer.

It is easy to say that the solution is to de-clutter, and a hundred self-help books focus on just this. For most people, this is sound advice. Tidy, sort, simplify and discard your belongings according to how and if you intend to use them, to give you a less cluttered space to live or work in. There are some, however, who find that their clutter is comforting and convenient, and if that sounds like you, then the most stressful aspect of your clutter will be some well-meaning author telling you to clear it up. So I shan't.

Ergonomics

Ergonomics is not about de-cluttering or even organising your workplace. It is a whole science of ensuring that your workplace and all of its equipment and technology are designed to fit comfortably with the way your mind and body work, naturally. Here are some examples of the things that an ergonomist (see Brilliant Resources at the end of this chapter for where to find advice) could help you with, that could help reduce your workplace stress. Many of them can also be susceptible to an objective re-evaluation and some common sense.

- Improved layout of your desk, workbench or office can resolve eye strain and headaches, back and neck ache, and repetitive strain discomfort and injuries.
- Better choice and adjustments of furniture can prevent hip, back, shoulder and neck problems.
- Adjustment of environmental controls can reduce eye strain (lighting), muscle tension (cold), headaches (cold, heat, humidity, noise).
- Changing the location and design of switches and indicators can reduce accident rates.
- Provision of appropriate equipment can address the risks (and fears) of muscle strain, trips and falls, or accidental damage.

Stimulus

However pleasant your working environment is, you will need a break. Getting out and about to take you away from your normal environment will help stimulate and refresh your senses and your mind, on top of the obvious benefit to your brain of the fresh air and exercise.

'Have nothing in your house that you do not know to be useful, or believe to be beautiful.'

William Morris

What William Morris is saying, simply, is fill your life with nice stuff. You may or may not be able to do this at work, but even in the most austere workplaces there is a tiny scope for some personalisation. If possible, create some sort of stimulus to prompt your best thinking and create the most conducive environment for yourself that you can.

When you can't, you need to create somewhere lovely and comforting and stimulating for yourself somewhere where you do have control: your home. For some people this is family photos, hand-me-down ornaments and comfy slippers. For others, it is natural objects, beautiful artwork and treasured books, or maybe a music system and some favourite recordings, or a cupboard full of cookery ingredients and measuring jugs. Whatever it is, make this your escape hatch to your own private world where you can do your own thing and gradually discharge your stress.

Your sensory environment: smells, noise, light and colour

Other aspects of your environment are equally important. In fact, one could argue that, as smell is our most primitive sense, plugged into the most fundamental part of our brains, this is more important to our wellbeing than almost anything. Yet how many of us give it more than a passing thought?

Smells

It is unlikely that you will be able to do much to control the smells in your workplace, but your home is yours to manage. There is a vast array of fragrance products on the market, but for real mastery of how scent affects mood, wellbeing and stress, we need to turn to the art of aromatherapy. Aromatherapists use essential oils derived from plant extracts to treat a range of ailments, using massage, baths or simply letting the scent infuse a room.

The last of these approaches is safe with most oils, but it is worth seeking expert advice, as many of the oils have potent effects and can be dangerous to some medical conditions. An example is clary sage which can cause problems for pregnant women and people with epilepsy.

brilliant list

Some essential oils widely recommended to help with aspects of stress

- Clary sage
- Geranium
- Lavender
- Mandarin
- Neroli
- Rose
- Sandalwood
- Ylang Ylang

Do consult an expert source for advice on which to use and how to use them.

Noise

The levels and types of noises in your environment can be either a stressor, or can help relieve your stress, so, once again, consider what you can do to adjust your sound environment. Here are three suggestions.

Do as you would be done by

Set the tone by adjusting your phone so that you don't have to shout to be heard, and keep desk or workstation conversations at a subdued level.

Block it out

In an industrial, construction or workshop setting, ear defenders may be a mandatory feature of health and safety precautions, but you may be able to request them (or buy your own) if they are not – as long as an inability to hear does not cause a safety risk. In an office environment, earplugs are a cheap and unobtrusive option – as long as you don't need to be able to hear a ringing phone. If you do, a visual cue extension, as used by people with hearing difficulties, is an option.

Many workplaces may frown on music headsets, but, if it is appropriate, you can design your sound-scape to meet your own preferences.

Cover it up

Some people have trouble sleeping or concentrating because of unwanted ambient noise, and radio or music will not help them. A solution is white noise – the hiss you get from a de-tuned FM radio. You can buy white noise generators, but why bother when you can just de-tune an FM radio! With the switch-over to digital radio in many countries, old FM radios will be easy to find and come ready de-tuned!

Classical music

Researchers from the University of California and Mount Sinai Medical Centre have shown that music can improve heart-rate recovery from stress. However, not all music selections are effective: it was classical music that caused blood pressure to drop faster in their research subjects. Of course, they only tried a limited number of selections (Pachelbel's 'Canon', and 'Spring' from Vivaldi's *Four Seasons*), and some classical music is unlikely to be relaxing, like large chunks of Wagner, but it does point you towards another resource.

Light

The brightness and quality (mixture of colours) of light can affect our moods, but there is one type of light that seems to have the greatest positive effect on our mood: natural daylight. There is even a mental health syndrome linked to wintertime, when there is less of it: seasonal affective disorder, sometimes known as SAD, or the winter blues. You cannot always get more daylight into your work space or home, but you can pop out at breaks to get some fresh air and daylight.

Colour

There is limited research on the effects of colour on our emotions, and most of it focuses on trying to understand how colour affects buying decisions. So we have to be careful about interpreting how colour in your environment will affect your stress levels and acknowledge that the one person who knows best is you.

That said, there is some interesting research by Naz Kaya and Helen Epps at the University of Georgia, where they asked people to rate the extent to which 13 different colours evoke each of 23 emotions (including 'no emotion'). Whilst these self-ratings did not measure actual emotions, the results are consistent with a lot of un-researched assertions and fragmentary research results on the effects of colour on mood. For us, the particularly relevant findings are:

- Green was most strongly associated with the emotions of 'confident' and 'peaceful'.

- Yellow was most strongly associated with the emotions of 'energetic' and 'happy'.

- Blue was most strongly associated with the emotion of 'calm'.

- Purple-blue was most strongly associated with the emotion of 'calm'.

- Blue-green was most strongly associated with the emotion of 'happy'.

A lot of other research seems to suggest that blues, greens and blue-greens may reduce stress and irritability, and induce relaxation. Studies have found that consumers feel more at ease in blue and green retail environments, which retailers want, as they are inclined to stay longer and spend more money.

Kaya and Epps were among many researchers who found one association to avoid:

- Green-yellow was most strongly associated with the emotions of 'sick' and 'disgusted'.

Action

Stress often comes from a mismatch of what you think about and what you do. So take control of your agenda, and focus your action on the things that are going on in your head. Put together a plan and set aside specific time to carry it out. The need to put it off because you don't have the time now will just reintroduce the stress unless you know that you have a specific slot in your diary to tackle it.

Unmade decisions are another source of stress. Make time to review the evidence and reflect carefully on important decisions, so that you can resolve the situation and move forward.

unmade decisions are another source of stress

brilliant tip

Making a decision that you have been putting off

If there is a decision that you have mentally put into your 'too difficult' box, it is probably competing with other things that are easier to do.

Step 1: Schedule a time when the decision is the only thing on your agenda.

Step 2: Write out clearly:

● The situation

● What is most important for you to achieve

● The options.

Step 3: Against each option, make a note of two things:

● The extent to which it addresses what is most important to you

● Your most serious reservations about it, including concerns about what could go wrong.

Step 4: Now you are ready to consider your decision with a clear head.

Escape

In Figure 1.4, we saw that there are two areas of worry that can cause us stress: the things you can control and the things you cannot. By focusing on the things that you can control, you will reduce your stress, but sometimes that zone feels too small: there is little or nothing that you are able to control.

You always have options. If your situation is putting your well-being or even, long term, your life at risk, then if you cannot control your situation, you must get away from it. Some of the people in Richard Logan's research gave themselves a sense of control in the most demanding of circumstances, not by controlling those circumstances but by plotting their escape.

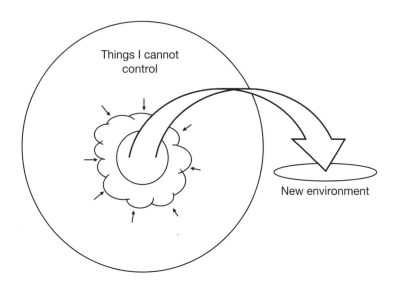

Figure 3.1 Escape from a situation you cannot control

🡵 brilliant resources

- In the UK, The Health and Safety Executive (HSE) is responsible for ensuring that work spaces are safe, and therefore can give some guidance on ergonomics: **www.hse.gov.uk**
- The Institute of Ergonomics and Human Factors can offer a wealth of advice and a list of registered experts and consultancies: **www.ergonomics.org.uk**

brilliant recap

- Taking control of your environment starts with believing that you can do it, and then making a commitment.

- People are an essential part of your environment, so select and protect your relationships.

- Being organised is one of the simplest ways to reduce your stress – and organising is a simple way to seize control.

- The physical space and environment you occupy can have a profound effect on your sense of wellbeing. Take some trouble to modify them to meet your personality and preferences.

- When you make a decision, you feel a sense of relief. If you cannot modify a stressful environment, then make the decision to get out.

CHAPTER 4

Control your time

Powerful time management is a learnable skill. Distinguish what is important from what is urgent, apply the 80:20 rule, find things you can defer, delegate or drop. This chapter will give you an overview of the basic principles of time management, so that you can once again feel in control of your time.

There is no single solution to time management; different techniques will work for different people. In *Brilliant Time Management*, the OATS Principle is used to draw together a lot of powerful techniques into a simple process. Here is a brief introduction.

The OATS Principle

Write it down

If you have a head full of things you need or want to do, this can cause you stress. Just by writing it all down, you can free up mental capacity without the worry that you will forget something important. Secondly, once you have written something down, it will take on a more objective level of importance in your mind. So, that job around the house that you have been telling yourself that you *must* do for the last year will start to look a whole lot more like a 'nice to do' job that you can schedule into a Sunday morning in the next couple of months.

The OATS Principle gives you a simple process for writing down and planning the things you need to do.

OATS

OATS stands for:

- Outcomes
- Activities
- Time
- Schedule

It sets out, in sequence, the four steps in planning how to use your time effectively. Some people will ask: *'When should I get my OATS?'* Well, if you ever have trouble sleeping at night because the things you need to do tomorrow are buzzing around in your head, then you should get your OATS before you go to bed. Otherwise, it is equally effective to do it in the morning, before you start your day's activities.

The next four sections of this chapter describe each of the steps in turn. Then we will turn to three of the commonest stress-inducing time management problems: putting things off, saying no, and dealing with a feeling of being overwhelmed. We will end on a lighter but crucial note: the importance of celebration.

Outcomes

The first step in OATS planning is to decide what you want to be different at the end of tomorrow or next week, next month or next year. These are your outcomes. From here on, we will illustrate OATS planning with a daily planning process, but you can plan your next week with it, or your next month, or even the next year. Keep the number of outcomes you set to a manageable number. For example, in one day, three would be a good number, but it is possible there may just be one thing you want to achieve. If you are getting past five, ask yourself: *'Am I just creating more pressure and stress than I need?'*

brilliant activity

Goal setting

Deciding your outcomes for the next day – or week or year – can be difficult. There are often so many competing demands on your time and attention. This is stressful, so really effective time management (rather than being reactive and managing the tasks you already have) requires a big picture of what you are trying to achieve in your life: your goals.

Put aside at least half an hour – more if you can – to sit quietly with a notepad, and think through the answers to these four questions:

1 *How is my life, now?*
   Inventory each aspect of your life: your family and friendships, your home life, your career and work life, your financial situation, your hobbies and interests, your education and self-development. How content and successful do you feel in each area, and overall? What are you happy with? What would you like to change, or develop?

2 *What is important to me?*
   Now think through what sort of person you really are. What words would you use to describe yourself? For example, you may be ambitious, arrogant, caring, dependable, enthusiastic, intellectual, jolly, miserly, practical, selfish … Pick a dozen or so words. Once you have done that, ask yourself: 'What things are most important to me in my life?'

3 *What do I want?*
   Such a simple question. Ask yourself what you want for yourself, what you want to achieve, and how you want your life to be in the future. What do you need to learn, to do, to acquire, to achieve? Write these down, because these are your goals in life.

4 *When do I want them?*
   Pursuing too many goals can be stressful, so start to prioritise and sequence them. For each goal, prioritise it as either primary (something you feel you must achieve to create fulfilment in your life) or secondary

(something that will add to your life). Then, starting with your primary goals, give each a timescale. Keep it simple, like one year, five years, 10 years or 20 years.

This work will form the basis from which you can start planning your time and evaluating the value of the possible outcomes you could set in your OATS planning.

Activities

Once you have your outcomes for tomorrow, the next thing to do is to list all of the things you need to do in order to achieve them. You may think that this just sounds like a 'To Do' list, but it isn't.

To Do lists

A To Do list is a long list of all of the things that you would like to do. You can prioritise them, you can set deadlines against them, and you can cross things off them, but you can rarely finish them. To Do lists have a habit of growing as fast as we get things done. Just restarting the list on a new sheet of paper does not detract from the essential nature of a To Do list: the better you are at using it, the faster you will add things to it. Since there's always more to do, the diligent time manager will never stop work, and the struggling time manager will rapidly feel overwhelmed. Either way, To Do lists are a common cause of stress.

> To Do lists have a habit of growing as fast as we get things done

To Day lists

When you add activities against each outcome in your OATS plan, you get a To Day list. Unlike its harmful cousin, it is a closed list: you can complete it and, having done so, feel good about yourself and stop working. The other advantage is that each activity is prequalified as important: it will help you achieve an outcome you have decided that you want, and that outcome will be linked to one of your goals.

Important or urgent?

President Eisenhower knew what it was to have a lot to do. He is commonly credited with a helpful insight:

'Most things which are urgent are not important, and most things which are important are not urgent.'

Attributed to Dwight D. Eisenhower

This insight has given rise to a very helpful time management tool, the Urgent–Important quadrants, illustrated in Figure 4.1.

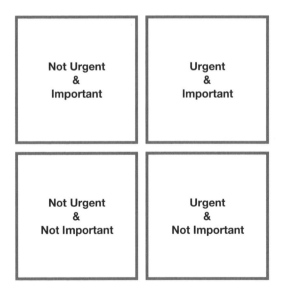

Not Urgent & Important	**Urgent & Important**
Not Urgent & Not Important	**Urgent & Not Important**

Figure 4.1 Urgent versus important

If you are able to assess separately what is urgent (subject to real time pressure) and what is important (with real consequences), you can start to prioritise the demands on your time. You can neglect things that are neither urgent nor important – and you should. Things that are urgent but not important can also be neglected, but if you do choose to do them, tackle them quickly and do not invest more time than you need to, to meet a minimum standard. Important and urgent things need your attention now, and you should give them all the time they need. Once you really gain control of your time, you will start to find your days filled with things that are important but not urgent.

They may have become urgent to you in the past, but you are now so 'in control', that you are getting them completed in good time, before they can become urgent and important. By now, you will find only one real criterion for assessing importance: *'How much can this activity contribute to my goals?'*

Time

Once you have a closed list of activities for the coming day, the next step is to estimate how long each one will take. You may not be good at estimating timings now, but if you get into the habit of doing it every time, you will find, almost magically, that you start to get better and better at it, as your brain starts to recognise patterns and home in on them.

Underestimation

Underestimating how long things will take is another cause of stress. As you near your estimated completion time and things aren't done yet, your body will start to react to the threat that this, and then the next thing, won't get done, and the possible consequences of incomplete activities and unrealised outcomes. This is especially so if you have been diligent in focusing on only important tasks, because these matter; they have consequences.

So, there are three ways to manage this risk, and effective time managers use all three in combination:

1 *Prioritise*

Even if everything you plan to do today is important, it is wise to assess which things are the most important, so that you can get them started early and allocate your most productive time to them – when you feel at your best and can work uninterrupted. Likewise, knowing what is least important (or least urgent) will give you the confidence to reschedule some activities to another day, if you need to, freeing up more time for the higher-priority tasks that are taking you longer than expected.

2 *Contingency*

Always add a little extra time to your estimates, to create some contingency. Add more contingency for unfamiliar or complex tasks, or tasks requiring contributions from other people, or other people's agreement.

3 *Breaks*

Allow time in your day for breaks. Not only will these keep you fresh and working at your most efficient levels, but, if you are under pressure, then you can use some of your break time to get more done. If you only schedule minimal breaks, you will not have this flexibility.

Schedule

The last step in OATS planning is to schedule your activities into your day. You will need to know any fixed commitments you have before you start, and, to do this well, it will help you to divide your activities into three categories, according to how substantial the tasks are.

Elephants, sheep and mice

Divide your activities into 'elephants', 'sheep' and 'mice'. Elephants are the biggest, most complex and demanding activities; sheep are of significant size, while mice are small, quick, easy tasks.

Start with the elephants. Schedule these into times of your day when you can give them your best and most focused attention. Choose times when you are at your best and are least likely to be disturbed. For me, writing this book is an elephant task, and I schedule it into the start of the morning, when I feel fresh, alert and am able to get things done before emails arrive and phones ring.

Then schedule the sheep into other times of the day when you are feeling good and can allocate a solid chunk of time to them. Finally, schedule the mice into the gaps between sheep and elephant tasks.

Reduce stress

Keep your stress levels low by also scheduling breaks for small pleasures and rewards that will help you relax and discharge any stresses and tensions. These can also act as contingencies, if important activities over-run.

Procrastination

A big source of stress is the inability to get started. We all put things off sometimes, but chronic procrastination adds the stress of feeling guilty to the stress of having a workload build up. Then, there is the stress of complaints about what you haven't done.

---

brilliant list

Ten quick tips for beating your urge to defer

1 Footprints
   Split the task into a series of small achievements, each of which you can easily attain.

2 Rewards

Promise yourself a reward for completing the task (and be sure you keep your promise).

3 Differently

Find a different way to do the activity; for example, instead of typing a letter, write it out in pencil if it's easier. Typing it will then be easier too.

4 Blitz

Set yourself a challenge to make as much progress as you can within the duration of an external event, like a TV ad break, a piece of music, while your partner is out shopping, or between now and leaving for a meeting.

5 Time-box

Set aside a specific time, like 20 minutes, to work on the task, with no anticipation of completing it. This will relieve performance pressure, and limit the time you spend doing something you don't like. And often, you'll get to the end of your time and be so near finishing that you'll want to carry on. Go for it!

6 Just one thing

Don't try to do the task: just do one small thing that gets it started. Instead of weeding the garden, go out and pull the weeds out of one small part of the path.

7 Dreaming

Fantasise about how good you will feel when the job is done. The more vivid and powerful you can make these emotions, the more desire you will have to get started. Visualise the task as being on one end of a piece of elastic, and pleasure on the other. Feel that elastic stretching …

8 Nothing else

Clear your workbench, clear your worktop, clear your desk. Hide your To Do list and put away anything that relates to any other task. Turn off any computer program that you don't need, and leave only one task available. With all of the other things you have to do out of the way, it is far easier to focus on the one thing that's been bugging you.

9   Promise
    Make someone a promise that you will get it done. Or two people, or
    three. The bigger the promise, the more you'll want to get on with it.

10 Bring it on
    If all else fails, get macho. Think about *I'm a Celebrity* … and the task of
    eating a live spider. Psych yourself up, open your mouth, and bring it on.

Say NO

Part of controlling stress is not exposing yourself to unnecessary
stressors, so a vital part of your time management toolkit is your
ability to say 'no'. Once you have
your goals and you know what is
important, then you should be able
to weed out the unimportant calls on
your time and decline them.

*a vital part of your time
management toolkit is
your ability to say 'no'*

Noble Objections

Saying 'no' is difficult for most of us, because it feels like we are
letting others down. 'No' is a negative word, and who likes to be
seen as negative? However, it is perfectly reasonable for you to
decide how you use your time, and therefore perfectly reasonable for you to say 'no' to unwanted demands.

So 'no' can be positive, when you say it for the right reasons.
Then it becomes noble: a Noble Objection to a proposal. Saying
'yes' to everything might be a great way to advance in the early
stages of a career, but it will rapidly bring diminishing returns.
No longer will people respect you more for saying 'yes': they will
respect you less. Too much 'yes' and you become a 'yes-man' or
'yes-woman' – treated like a doormat by anyone who wants a
mug to do something for them.

On the other hand, when you get a reputation for saying yes
selectively, to important things; and that reputation is backed up

by a 100 per cent record of delivering on your commitments to the highest standards, then people will really respect and value you. So don't just say 'no' to unimportant tasks; make a Noble Objection: say 'NO'.

Delegation

Once you can gracefully decline responsibilities and work from other people, the next skill to learn is how to delegate some of *your* work to others. This can be good for you and also good for them, but only when you delegate carefully. Here is how to do so, in five easy stages.

Matching

Carefully match the task to the person. Choose someone who can learn from the task, or gain confidence or recognition from doing it. There must be something in it for me, if I am to take on a task for you willingly. If, on the other hand, you simply dump the jobs you don't fancy, or set people up to fail, they will soon come to resent you.

Briefing

If you are delegating to me, then brief me well. Let me know the background, so I can understand the context of the task, and what you expect of me. You may want to set me objectives in terms of what you want, the standards I must meet, any deadlines or timescales, and the budget or resources that I have available. Be really clear about the level of authority that you are delegating to me. For example, are you leaving every decision to me, to do the whole job and report back when it's done, or do you need to be involved in key decisions? How do you want me to report back to you during and after my work? Finally, think carefully about how much advice you give me on how to do the job. Find a good balance between giving me too much guidance and thus stifling my creativity and robbing me of the learning experience of figuring it out for myself; and giving me too little guidance and leaving me anxious and exposed, with a risk to me, to the organisation, and to you, if I get something wrong.

Commitment

Check that I understand what you want, am able to do it, and am committed to taking it on. In return, give me your commitment to provide me with the support I need, to do the job well, to do it safely, and to learn from my experience.

Monitoring

The task started off as yours, so the ultimate responsibility for it – and now for me – lies with you. So, periodically, check in with me to find out how I am doing and give me the support I need. Set the frequency and style of your monitoring to match the level of risk, the importance of the task and my needs for support and guidance.

Feedback

When I am finished, review my performance. Give me good feedback on what I have done, that will help me learn and build my confidence. Thank me for my work and give me praise for what I have done well.

Dealing with overwhelm

Sometimes there is just too much to do and you are frozen by a feeling of being overwhelmed by it all. You need to grasp control and here is a simple five-point plan to do just that.

1 Make a list of all the things that are overwhelming you

This will look like a To Do list, and it is important to get everything down so that you can manage the problem.

2 Apply the Urgent and Important categories

For each task, assess whether it is urgent or not and whether it is important or not. Now be bold: delete every task that is not important. If this feels just a little too scary, before you delete them, place them on to a new list: a To Don't list. You can then file this away so that you won't lose sight of those tasks, but, equally, they won't distract you from the important ones.

3 Divide the remainder into three lists

A **Urgent and Important and quick (Type A)**
These are the things you can do in a few minutes.

B **Urgent and Important and substantial (Type B)**
These are the things that will need some focused effort.

C **Important but Not Urgent**
These are the things to save until you no longer feel overwhelmed.

4 Clear the Urgent and Important things first

Use the 'Boxed Burst and Break' (BB+B) method:

1 **Frenzy**
Allow exactly 15 minutes to clear all the quick things (Type A) you can.

2 **Burst of work**
Now do 40 minutes of intense work on one of the more substantial things (Type B). Aim to make some real progress in a strict 40-minute slot.

3 **Now take a break for five minutes**
This must include one glass of water and some time outside in the fresh air.

5 Repeat step 4

Continue the BB+B method until you feel in control of your task lists and you are no longer overwhelmed. Take a more substantial break after three or four cycles. You will probably find that you clear all of your quick, Type A tasks before you have finished your Type B tasks. If you are still in overwhelm, then skip the Frenzy step and allow 50-minute bursts of work on your Type B tasks, with 10-minute breaks.

Celebration

If you want to break the cycle of success, it is vital that you recognise progress, so that your brain can start to stand down its fight-or-flight troops. So, make a point of noticing and acknowledging your successes. Praise yourself and celebrate your achievements. Even give yourself little rewards. Noticing your successes will change your stress levels all on its own.

Take your time

As you start to bring your time under control, mastery will come when you start to slow down and take your time over things.

There is an old proverb: *'more haste, less speed'*. Who knows if it's true? It certainly seems to be. What is true, however, is that taking the time to be present in the moment, to savour the sounds, colours and textures around you, to relish the company you are in, or to enjoy the flavours of your food, will relax you. Make time for good company, make time for your loved ones, and make time for yourself. These are the ultimate rewards of good time management.

make time for good company, make time for your loved ones, and make time for yourself

brilliant recap

- For brilliant time management, get your OATS.
- Don't put things off – you'll only end up wasting more time, feeling guilty, and getting more stressed.

- Say NO when it is the noble thing to do.
- When too many things overwhelm you, use the structured Boxed Burst and Break method to take control.
- Celebrate your successes, so you know you are making progress.

CHAPTER 5

Control your attitudes

What is important to you?

What is really important to you?

What things drive the decisions you make in your life?

One of the major sources of stress is a conflict between these values and some of the requirements that work, or our relationships, or our other choices put upon us. Sometimes it's a conflict between our values and what we are asked to do, sometimes it's a conflict with the values of our employer, and sometimes it's a conflict with the values of the people around us: our bosses, colleagues, customers, family members or social contacts. Sometimes it's a conflict with the values that we believe will make us successful.

Values conflict is a particular source of stress at work. It may be deep-seated and the only way to resolve it is to find different work. However, there may be another solution. We all

> values conflict is a particular source of stress at work

want to live by our values, but very few of us actually set out to choose them. Have you ever taken time to articulate what your values are, let alone what you want them to be?

Sometimes your acquired values drive you to make choices that serve you poorly. Perhaps those values did serve you well once.

Now you are stuck with them – rather like the way you are stuck with your fight-or-flight response, even though it was designed for an ancient environment. The difference is: you can change your values, because they are not part of you. Rather, most of us got them from our parents, our society, our schooling and our religion.

The iceberg model

A compelling way to think of your values, and why they are so important, is to picture yourself as an iceberg. What people see of you is the part that is above the water: your behaviour and the effect you have on the world, as a result. Below the water line are aspects of you that nobody can see: your capabilities, the beliefs you have about yourself and the world, and the values that drive you. Deepest of all is your sense of who you are.

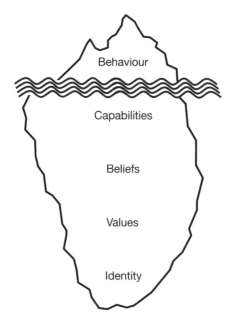

Figure 5.1 The iceberg model

Your values set out what is important to you in life, and when they interact with your beliefs about yourself and the world they combine to create a powerful set of drivers that, mostly unconsciously, control many aspects of your behaviour.

Some of these drivers set up stresses and strains in us as we pursue unhelpful behaviours. Some of your values set up stresses and strains because they conflict with the values of the people you have chosen to spend time with and organisations you have chosen to be a part of.

The next two sections of this chapter focus on the attitudes and beliefs that drive you, and on what you want and how that derives from your values. The two sections that follow show you how you can seize control of the whole underwater part of the iceberg, building confidence and assertiveness, and knowing what you are entitled to in life. This is important, as it is not the wind above the water that determines where an iceberg will go, but the currents under the water.

Dangerous attitudes and limiting beliefs

Let's examine some of the unconscious attitudes and ways of thinking that drive behaviours and can lead to unwanted stress. Each of these drivers results from your subconscious mind believing that you will only be a good person if you do certain things. So you do them to protect yourself, only to find that there is a price to pay.

Please others

Abdus feels a strong need to please the people around him. This creates a burden of responsibility that means he rarely feels able to do things for himself. He is always thinking: 'When I've done this, then I can …' This makes Abdus a good team player and a caring family man, but also means he puts his own feelings very much in second place to those of the people around him.

Abdus's need to please may have served him well in the past, getting him to where he is now. But now there are just too many things you say 'yes' to and that just leaves him exhausted, anxious to do everything, guilty when he can't and, overall, unnecessarily stressed.

Not only can it be stressful for Abdus to continually please others, but he rarely gets a chance to unwind and do things for himself. If you are like Abdus, then learn to say 'NO' from time to time, and create opportunities to please yourself. Have the confidence to know that others will respect you for who you are – valuing your integrity, not just your willingness to please them. People may like you at first but it is very easy to become a doormat – taken for granted and never noticed. Now all you have left is the fear that, if you don't please them, they will turn on you.

---

7 brilliant technique

SCOPE the problem

Whenever someone asks you to do something, before you instinctively say 'yes' to try to please them:

- **Stop**

    Take a moment to evaluate the situation.

- **Clarify**

    What do they want?

- **Options**

    What could you do in response? How effective would different responses be? What choice will you make – willingly?

- **Proceed**

    Give your response.

- **Evaluate**

When you get a moment, review the interaction dispassionately and evaluate the extent to which you felt in control of your response. What would you want to do if the same situation arose next time?

Pleasing others leads them to like us, but the value they put on help so freely given can be temporary and the respect they give shallow. Please yourself more. Do what is important to you, not to other people. When helping out or building a relationship is important to you, then choose to do it. This way others will recognise that your true contribution is to focus on doing the right things, and they will value you accordingly.

Try harder

Bella wants to feel she deserves a rest, but she won't let up. Consequently, she ends up too exhausted to either enjoy her rest or really benefit from it. She takes on far too much and often seems to repeat yesterday's mistakes. She feels it was drummed into her by her parents and by her school. If she works harder, she will be rewarded better; she will feel more deserving and get more leisure and pleasure.

Bella deserves a rest and, if you are like her, so do you. So take it when you feel the need – or even the desire. Overwork is not a virtue: nobody ever says that they wished they'd worked harder, as they lie dying.

If you continually drive yourself to work harder, you risk exhaustion, depression, and a complete lack of fulfilment from your success. To achieve more, work smarter. Manage your time and your priorities and optimise the way you do things. SCOPE your opportunities and see what you can do to achieve more by doing less. You want to feel that you deserve what you earn – but please allow yourself the time to enjoy it. Work smart and spend more time at home and at play.

A hard-working executive spent his holiday near an African fishing village. Every morning, he saw a little fishing boat return to the quayside. One day, he asked the fisherman how long it took to catch his fish.

'Not very long,' answered the fisherman.

'Then, why didn't you stay out longer and catch more?'

The fisherman explained that his catch was enough for his family, so the executive asked, *'But what do you do with the rest of your time?'*

'I sleep late, play with my children, doze in the afternoon under a palm tree, and go to the bar with my friends, have a few beers, play music, and sing songs. I have a good life,' replied the fisherman.

The executive was horrified at the waste: *'I have an MBA from Harvard and I can help you. You should start by fishing longer every day. You can then sell the extra fish you catch. With the proceeds, buy a bigger boat. This will bring extra money, so you can buy a second and a third one, and hire men, until you have a large fleet. Instead of selling at market, you can negotiate directly with the processing plants. Eventually you can open your own plant. You can then leave this village and move to the city, and get an office to direct your business from.'*

'How long would that take?' asked the fisherman.

'You will need a 20-year business plan,' replied the executive.

'And what will I do when my business gets really big?' asked the fisherman.

'Then you will be able to spend your weekends at a small village by the sea, sleep late, spend time with your family, go fishing, take afternoon naps, and have relaxing evenings drinking and making music with your friends.'

Be perfect

Clifford is always critical of himself, never feeling that what he has done is good enough. He has little rituals that he pursues almost compulsively, feeling agitated if they get interrupted. This makes Clifford prone to working later, trying to polish the reports he writes and get every table in them exactly right. It also causes friction with co-workers, because nothing they do ever seems to meet Clifford's exacting standards. Things have to be 'just right'. Don't call him Cliff!

If you are like Clifford, then you need to realise that you are good enough as you are. When you settle for less, sometimes you can achieve more. Rather than always aim for the gold standard, start out by thinking through *'What is "good enough" in this situation – what should "finished" look like?'*

Be strong

Devla likes to be on her own and is uncomfortable with large groups. Their pointless chit-chat does not come easily to her. Instead, she hides her feelings and can even withdraw from her friends – especially at times of stress. The last thing that she would want is for them to see her weakness, and she would never feel comfortable asking for help.

Asking for support can feel risky but, if she doesn't, Devla will only end up exhausting herself, feeling all alone and angry, with no one to turn to.

If you are a little like Devla, then you want to show your independence, but do you really want to be alone? Find someone that you can be honest with, and express what you need and what you want. People want to help, and most people will do more for those they love than they will do for themselves. You would always help those you love, so allow them to do as much for you.

> you would always help those you love, so allow them to do as much for you

Hurry up

Enrique is always rushing around, but he never seems to be particularly effective. He won't plan, so is constantly surprised by events, and then rarely does anything he is proud of because he is too focused on whatever is next. At the back of his mind, Enrique is thinking: *'If I don't get a move on, something bad will happen – and it will be my fault.'*

Slow down, Enrique: take your time. If you are like him, then take a moment to think about the Urgent and Important boxes you read about in Chapter 4. You probably spend all of your time focused on the Urgent things, often letting the Urgent and Not Important things compete with the Urgent and Important.

When you take time to plan ahead, you will find two things:

1   You will be better able to spot the Urgent and Not Important things and make a conscious decision to drop them or at least leave them until after the Important things are done.

2   You will start to have fewer things in your life that are Urgent and Important. You will find yourself dealing with them before they get urgent.

Be careful

Funmi wants to feel safe, and so will take no risks. Her work is okay, but not special, so, despite her being diligent and bright, her less-able colleagues get promoted ahead of her. With total safety comes boredom: Funmi is not growing in her role, learning or taking on challenges. She is getting bored, and all that leaves her almost paralysed by fear of making a mistake and losing what she has.

What is really the worst that can happen for Funmi? If you are a bit like her, evaluate the possible outcomes objectively, then look for ways to control the risks that there are. You may not yet be ready for your first free-fall jump, but you might just feel safe enough to try the climbing wall at your local leisure centre.

Try things out

'You want to feel safe – but what would you do if you knew you could not fail?'

When you find the answer to that question, you know your life's goal.

Be right

Gene wants to be right, because he cannot face looking foolish. This makes him argumentative and pedantic or, at times, freezes him with indecision.

Gene needs to believe that it is okay to make mistakes. Each one is a lesson for him, and what is really important is that he learns the lessons and avoids repeating the same mistake. Making mistakes is a far more effective learning mechanism than getting things right; it is the principal way toddlers learn.

If you also feel the need to be right all of the time, then let yourself make some mistakes. Expect some frustrations, failures and sorrows; accept them, live with them, and move on.

brilliant tip

If you want to be right all of the time, then always be prepared to listen and observe objectively, learn from the situation and then change your mind if your were wrong at the start.

Be serious

Hetal wants to be respectful and respected, and so comes across as a very serious person; humourless, in fact. People find it hard to connect with her, and she finds it hard to talk about anything but 'issues that matter'.

But who says she can't be playful as well?

Feel guilty

Isaac wants to do the right thing, but gets things wrong sometimes. He apologises profusely, but carries the memory for hours, days or even weeks sometimes, building up a bank of guilt for all of the inevitable accidents, mistakes and unintended discourtesies that we all commit.

If you are like Isaac, then you know that you will make mistakes. Acknowledge them, learn from them and, in the words of American folk wisdom:

''Fess up – say sorry – move on.'

Know what you want

Your most fundamental attitude is to know what you want. It links your values to who you are. Values are hard to define, but at their simplest they are the criteria that lead you to the decisions that you want to make. They are an expression of the models of the world that you hold most dear, and so define what is really important to you.

Your values

When your values conflict with the values of the people around you and their expectations of you, you want to rebel. Where you feel unable to do so – because you feel tied into a relationship or you feel you cannot afford to lose the job you hold, for example – then that conflict will cause stress. To relieve the stress, you must either change your values or change your situation.

We looked at changing your situation in Chapter 3, so let's now look at changing your values. Nobody has a right to expect you to change your values; neither your employer nor your spouse, nor anyone else. The only person who does have that right is you.

Yet, few of us even consider either what our values are or, less, how we might change them. Most have come to us by absorption from our environment – particularly in our childhoods and early adulthood. Socrates said that *'the unexamined life is not worth living'*. Philosophers may argue about what exactly he meant by this: characteristically, it has many interpretations from *'I would rather die than give up philosophy'* to *'If I don't appreciate my life, it has no value.'* One reading is that the only life worth living is one where we set our own rules.

brilliant exercise

Understanding and renewing your values

1 Pick the context in which you want to examine your values, for example, your values around your work and career, or your home and family life, or money, or health and fitness. Write this area of your life at the top of a page of notepaper.

2 Below this, write *'My values in this part of my life are:'* then list your values. To help you find your values, consider these questions:

   ● *'What's important to me about ...?'*

   ● *'If I had everything I want, what would cause me to give it all up?'*

   ● *'If that happened, what would cause me to keep everything?'*

3 Rank your values to establish an order of priority and number your values 1, 2, 3 ... To help you, consider these questions:

   ● *'Of these values, which is the most important to me?'*

▶

- 'Of the other values, which is the most important to me?'
- 'Why is this important to me?'

4 Review your list and ask yourself where each value comes from, and whether it is still a value you would like to have in your life. To help you, consider these questions:

- 'Did I choose this value, or did I get it from my parents, friends, teachers, colleagues ... ?'
- 'How much do I want this value to drive my choices in life?'
- 'What choices would be open to me if I changed this value?'

5 Give yourself permission to start to make any changes that you want.

- For each value that you want to retain, think: 'This value has served me well, and will continue to serve me well. I honour it.'
- For each value that you want to change, think: 'This value has served me well in the past, but I have changed. This is no longer a value I wish to direct my life, and I set it aside.'
- For each new value that you wish to adopt, think: 'This new value is one I freely choose. I will hold it for as long as it serves me well.'

You will be at your happiest when your values and your purpose in life support one another. Once again, however, too many of us commit our lives to what is expected of us, and not what we want.

Your life project

Human beings, unlike much of the animal kingdom, are motivated by so much more than opportunistic striving to survive: we feel a deep need to express who we are. As we grow up, we do this in different ways, eventually settling on our goals in life, and what we see as our vocation and purpose. We might call this your 'life project'.

An authentic life project

Stress arises when your life project is 'inauthentic'. That is, it is one that you feel you ought to pursue, in order to conform to the pressures and expectations of society, your family or other people around you. Such a role in life is almost predetermined for you by others and you will therefore have no motivation of your own to pursue it. The extent to which you do will be determined by the strength of your drivers to work hard, please others, be perfect, be careful and hurry up about it too!

You will be far happier and less stressed when you pursue an 'authentic' project: one you determined for yourself from a considered evaluation of your experiences. This will result in a decision freely made, and you will feel powerfully motivated when you work on it. Progress will be enormously satisfying.

Decide what you want from life: what will give you fulfilment and make you happy? Set yourself goals that enhance your life, and start to notice all of the opportunities that are available to help you meet your goals.

Too often, we put our goals far out into the future. Bring some of them forward and decide how to achieve some of them now. Some people spend a lot of time saying *'when I have some free time ...'* or *'when I retire ...'* If it's important to you, start now. Your hobbies, your pastimes, your very passions are massively empowering when you pursue them with vigour. Making time for what you really love to do is one of the best ways to reduce your feelings of stress.

From myths to mastery

Can someone else make you feel good? For that matter, can they make you feel bad? Most of us recognise times when a careless word or a deliberate insult has left us feeling awful, yet Eleanor Roosevelt said: *'No one can make you feel inferior without your permission.'*

The belief that other people can make you feel good or bad, by what they say, is just a myth. How you interpret their words is entirely up to you: *'Sticks and stones may break my bones but words can never hurt me.'*

Immunity to words

To be immune from taunts and insults, you need a strong positive self-image, which comes from valuing yourself and accepting your weaknesses yourself. Good self-esteem is an important asset in controlling stress. To help build up your self-esteem, here is a great exercise.

brilliant exercise

Self-esteem book

Buy yourself a small notebook – small enough to keep hidden, and to take with you when away from home overnight.

Each evening, take five minutes to write down three things that you have achieved today, or that you are proud of, or that you have contributed to in a positive way. These can be very small achievements or storming successes. What is important is that you do this regularly and keep it up until you start to feel really good about who you are and what you can do.

Self-confidence

Your self-esteem exercise will start to build up your confidence levels. To create a managed programme of confidence building, there are three further things you can do.

1 Seek out opportunities to take on challenges that will stretch you to do something beyond what you have done before. As you start to master your new level of performance, notice and acknowledge it. Put it into your Self-esteem book.

2 Start to find people whom you like and respect, who are successful and confident. Spend time with them, observing what they do and how they do it. What do you learn? Try out some of the things they do for yourself and, when it goes well, record it in your Self-esteem book.

3 Learn to manage your emotional response to challenging and stressful situations, to remove the feelings that undermine your confidence. This is such an important area that the whole of the next chapter is devoted to it.

Asserting yourself

Assertiveness is all about respect. If I respect myself more than I respect you, then my behaviour is likely to be aggressive when I feel under stress. If, however, I respect you more than I respect myself, then, under pressure, I am likely to adopt a passive approach. Assertive behaviour comes from a balance of respect for yourself and for others.

> assertive behaviour comes from a balance of respect for yourself and for others

When you behave assertively, you:

- Act on what is important to you
- Prioritise important relationships
- Say what you think and feel
- Collaborate and ask for help
- Do what is right, not what is easy
- Say 'NO' with confidence.

Three steps to saying NO

1 Acknowledge the request.

2 Make your Noble Objection (NO).

3 Offer appropriate suggestions or alternatives.

Assertiveness techniques

Aside from the ability to say 'NO', there is a wide range of ways to be assertive. Here are just a few.

Acknowledgement and honesty

Listen to a request and acknowledge that you have understood it. Then consider and express honestly what you think of it or how you feel about it, before giving your final answer.

Broken record

If someone resists your reasonable requirement of them, patiently and calmly repeat it again … and again. Avoid getting caught up in irrelevant reasons or personal attacks, and leave them unanswered. Stick to your message.

Dealing with criticism

Whether it's called feedback or criticism, sometimes you know it is just a means of attack. Keep the moral high ground by thanking the other person for their comment and asking for detail or evidence. This will soon expose whether they have observed a genuine shortcoming that you can learn from, or are simply trying to make you feel inferior.

Give something back

If someone rejects your NO, then show how reasonable you are by thinking through some alternatives that they could pursue. This shows you to be logical and reasonable.

Handling aggression

Knee-jerk reactions to aggression lead to either a passive response or an escalation of that aggression. SCOPE the situation. Think to yourself: '*I can handle this calmly.*' Here are nine responses that you can use individually and in combination, to deal with a series of aggressive reactions:

- Basic: state your point of view.
- Responsive: invite more clarification.
- Empathy: express your understanding of how the other person is feeling.
- Logical: point out the logic of what they are saying – or the flaws in their facts or analysis.
- Emotional: let them know how you feel to invite empathy from them.
- Consequences: point out what their aggression will mean.
- Arbitration: suggest seeking an independent person to give an objective opinion.
- Mediation: suggest seeking an independent person to facilitate a resolution.
- Disengagement: remember, if the aggression starts to look as if it could become violent, step away: '*I don't feel able to give you a response that will satisfy you, now. Let's resume this conversation tomorrow/in a couple of hours.*'

Chapter 9 covers the topic of conflict in greater detail.

brilliant recap

Your own bill of rights

- You are good enough as you are.
- You have the right to please yourself.
- You have the right to just do it and then stop.

- You have the right to ask for what you want.
- You have the right to take your time.
- You have the right to take a chance.
- You have the right to be wrong sometimes.
- You have the right to apologise and then move on.
- You have the right to have fun.
- You have the right to say NO.
- You have the right to make decisions that accord with your values.
- You have the right to pursue the projects you choose.
- You have the right to reject insults and unfounded criticism.
- You have the right to respect yourself.
- You have the right to be assertive.
- You have the right to step away from aggression.

CHAPTER 6

Control
your mental
response to
stress

Grant me the serenity to accept the things I cannot change;
The courage to change the things I can.

'The Serenity Prayer' by Reinhold Niebuhr

We saw this quote at the start of Chapter 3, where we started to look at *how* to change the things you can. Chapter 3 was about how to change your environment, Chapter 4 was about how to change the way you use your time, and Chapter 5 was about how to change your attitudes. This chapter will address the other part of the quote: how to accept the things you cannot change. We will concentrate on how to control the way you respond mentally and emotionally to stress.

Perhaps the most influential researcher in this area is Barbara Frederickson. She is widely credited with being one of the key thinkers in the establishment of 'Positive Psychology'. Whilst this name may sound a little self-help/new-age, this became a respected part of psychology in 1998, when President of the American Psychological Association, Martin Seligman, officially launched Positive Psychology as a distinct branch of psychology, and lifted it from the level of pop psychology to a topic of serious scientific research.

Frederickson showed how positive thoughts and experiences can undo negative emotions, make us more resilient to stress, and give us more choices both behaviourally and emotionally. When psychologists are talking of resilience, they mean pretty much what common usage would lead us to expect: that we can withstand and recover from harmful forces.

This chapter will highlight five mental approaches to building your resilience:

1 *Focus.* In any situation, we focus on one or a few aspects, because our brains are not capable of giving complete attention to everything. Our choice of which aspects can dictate how we interpret and therefore respond to the situation.

2 *Optimism.* Perhaps the fundamental attitude that resilient people have is the optimism that things will get better. We'll see why this is not just a blind faith in events, but a positive strategy for coping.

3 *Determination, flexibility and persistence.* This may be three things in one section, but they are intimately linked. Watch a healthy toddler trying to figure out how to build a tower from blocks, and then disrupt their play. They will show all three of these.

4 *Gratitude.* Some of the most astonishing yet unsurprising research shows the power of gratitude to help us to cope with adversity and feel better. We'll look at how to build this into your daily routine.

5 *Self-talk.* Yes, I know you talk to yourself; we all do. But what do you say when you are under stress? By making changes here, you can get a huge boost in your outlook, emotions and resilience.

Focus

A truism in life is that 'you get what you look for'. It is certainly true that our prejudices predispose us to see in people or events the things that we expect, because they cause our brains to filter out contrary evidence. So, what you focus on is vital.

If you expect a meeting or interview to go badly and to put you under pressure, then you brain will spot every expression, every choice of words and every action that could be interpreted as hostile and bring it to your attention, drowning out all of the neutral and positive comments or acts. If, on the other hand, you have prepared well, are confident, and expect the meeting to go well, then the first smile you get will reinforce this and odd choices of words will go unnoticed or be attributed to momentary lapses.

In a very real sense, our brains create our own reality for us, which may or may not correspond with what an objective observer might describe.

Meaning

'Take nothing on its looks; take everything on evidence. There's no better rule.'

The lawyer, Jaggers, in Charles Dickens's *Great Expectations*

Jaggers's injunction is an ideal. Yet, for most of the time we do exactly the opposite and interpret things as they seem. External events don't have any 'meaning'. They are what they are, and any meaning comes from the interpretations that you or I attach to them. How often have you heard yourself saying something like:

- *'When she says that, she doesn't think I'm good enough for ...'*
- *'When he does that, it means he thinks ...'*
- *'Did you see what she just did? She's a complete ...'*
- *'He didn't need to do that, he must want ...'*
- *'When that happens, it happens because ...'*

All of these sorts of thoughts involve either reading someone's mind, ascribing meaning to an action or event, or assuming a reason that may be completely false. When we get stressed, objectivity and reason easily give way to this kind of thinking.

 **activity**

Recover your perspective

When you hear your inner voice making statements like these, SCOPE the situation:

Stop   Listen to the voice and stop it.

Clarify   What exactly are you thinking? What interpretation are you putting on the events around you?

Options   What alternative interpretations are available to you? Compare each one with the real evidence. Don't be afraid to acknowledge (and this is often the case) that you really do not have enough evidence to know what the underlying truth is.

Proceed   Act not on your first instinct, but on your best considered instinct.

Evaluate   Constantly reassess new information and test it against possible interpretations. As the evidence changes, then change your interpretation accordingly.

Choose to accept or choose to reject

One of the clearest examples of our tendency to put our focus in the wrong place is when somebody's chance remark (or even a spiteful comment) makes us feel bad for the rest of the day.

'No one can make you feel inferior without your consent.'

Eleanor Roosevelt

The possibility that *I* can make you feel good or bad, just by what I say, is a myth. But it is true that *you* can make yourself feel good or bad by how you choose to deal with what I say. The importance of making a conscious choice was best captured two and a half thousand years ago, by Buddha's problem of the gift. Buddha asked: *'If I offer you a gift and you refuse to accept it, who owns the gift?'*

Lead the mind: lead the body

brilliant exercise

Imagine you are holding a big, ripe, juicy, gorgeous orange. Hold out your hand and picture the orange in your hand. Feel its weight, see the shine and texture of its skin, smell the sharp sweetness. Now imagine that, in your other hand, you are taking a sharp knife. Bring it up to the orange, and just let it touch the skin. As it does so, imagine that tiny spray of zest and smell the sharp, intensely orange aroma of it. Now imagine cutting carefully into the flesh. The juices start to run, and they smell really sweet. When they touch your hand, they feel cold and sticky, and you know that this is going to be a lovely, juicy, sweet orange. Imagine you have cut it carefully right in half. Put the knife down safely and bring your orange up to your mouth. Imagine you are just about to take a bite and suck on the gorgeous sweet juices. The smell is intense now and you can feel the cool fresh juice running down your arm. Get ready to put the orange to your lips and STOP.

Is your mouth watering?

There is no orange. Yet most people who immerse themselves in the paragraph in the box above will experience their mouth water, as if there were. Your brain is the most powerful tool you have – and it controls your whole being. If your brain can do that with a fantasy orange, just think of all that it can do to control your response to stress if you let it.

focus on your points
of control and your
successes

So, focus on the good things that happen, rather than on the bad things. Focus on your points of control and your successes, and attach no more significance to events than they really deserve. What you focus on will influence your whole response to stressful events.

One of my Aikido teachers used to say: '*Lead the mind: lead the body.*' In martial arts, if you can direct your opponent's attention, you can easily control their body.

For example, the fundamental source of our stress-inducing fight-or-flight response is fear. In our modern context, one of the commonest forms of fear, whether we acknowledge it or not, is fear of failure. However, if we focus on all our advantages, the benefits of success, the resources we have and how we can plan and manage our success, we find our confidence grows and our fear diminishes – your stress response along with it.

Here is an exercise that harnesses your brain's ability to change how you feel, which we saw at the start of this section with the orange.

brilliant exercise

This exercise will help you to reduce the impact of stressors and regain a sense of calm control. This is an exercise to come back to whenever you need it, so practise it so that you can do it quickly and easily whenever you want to.

Think of something that you associate with stress. Picture it in your mind, as if it is an image on a television screen. Close your eyes and watch it on TV and, as you watch, imagine the TV starts to move further and further away from you, and the image gets dimmer and less distinct. Keep the TV moving away slowly and steadily, and the image getting fuzzier and dimmer, until, gradually, you can barely make out the image at all. Then, in your mind, get up and walk away.

Now open your eyes and think about your next meal. Yum.

When you are ready, next think of a time when you felt calm, confident and relaxed; and visualise that in your mind's eye. Put it on a TV screen as before and close your eyes. This time, imagine the TV is coming towards you and the image is getting bigger, clearer, brighter and more real. The colours are getting sharper and more vivid and it starts to feel like 3D TV. As the image gets bigger, feel it start to wrap around you so that you are immersed in it. When you feel ready, imagine yourself step into the image and take a deep breath. Aaahh.

Dealing with rage

Rage is like falling off a cliff. If stress moves you, step by step, towards the edge, it can take only one tiny shove to push you over the edge. Fortunately, we can usually detect the upwelling of anger that signals impending rage, so here are five things you can do when you sense your cork is about to pop.

1. Breathe

As we get tense and feel enraged, our bodies breathe more quickly and less deeply. This deprives you of oxygen, reducing your ability to think clearly. Deliberately reverse this by taking several deep breaths. Not only will this refill your lungs with fresh oxygen, but the action will send calming signals to your brain.

2. Smile

The world may not always smile with you, but your brain will. The act of smiling sends happy signals to your brain that will damp down your fight-or-flight response and so start to defuse your rage.

3. Get perspective

Mentally step away from the situation and see it objectively. When you try to analyse something, you will activate the logical front part of your brain, stealing some of the energy from your emotional brain centre. What is the real situation? How much does it really matter? How would you view it in a week's time, or in a year? Use the SCOPE process.

4. Step into their shoes

If it is someone else that has angered you, take a moment to step back and see the situation from their perspective. In their mind, what they did was totally reasonable. When you see things from their point of view, they will seem more reasonable and less enraging.

5. Make it absurd

If all else fails, activate your Monty Python organ – your ability to see the absurdity in any situation. Imagine the person who is annoying you is wearing ridiculous underwear, that their hair is just a wig, covering green hair, or that they are being unreasonable because they are desperate for the toilet. If it's an object that's causing you to explode, like a tangled ball of string, a part of your DIY project that's going wrong, or your computer playing up, imagine it has a voice, and speaks like a cartoon character; picture yourself painting it in a stupid colour for retribution; or imagine how it would look if you put it in the oven for an hour.

Optimism

An optimistic outlook is a huge asset. This is not about blindly believing that things will work out. This is about looking for opportunities that will create a good outcome, and about recognising your strengths and resources, and building on them.

Glass half full

'Glass-half-full' optimism is about seeing the bright side of everything and, by extension, ignoring the problems. '*An optimist,*' some say, '*differs from a pessimist because they are not in possession of all of the facts.*' Glass-half-full optimism is shallow; it is not enough.

Three real differences distinguish optimists from pessimists: their attitudes to fault, to permanence, and to responsibility.

Fault

A pessimist, prone to stress, will assume that whatever goes wrong is somehow *their* fault. An optimist will recognise that most events or failures are not their fault and, indeed, many are nobody's fault at all. Where something *is* their fault, rather than dwell on the failing, they seek to learn from it, put it right, and move on.

Permanence

Another distinction is in how optimists and pessimists take a long view of setbacks. An optimist will see any setback as temporary; something that, with the right effort and enough support and time, can be reversed. Pessimists see setbacks as part of an inevitable pattern that will persist indefinitely – or at least until their luck changes.

Responsibility

This is the big one. The optimist accepts responsibilities for their actions, but thereby takes responsibility for their future. This is the reason why optimism is such a powerful component of stress management: by taking responsibility, you give yourself the power to control your future; you seize control. A pessimist believes some outside agency – luck, other people, the establishment, or a god – has it in for them and that anything that goes wrong is outside their control.

> by taking responsibility, you give yourself the power to control your future

Tune your antennae

If you know what you want, and you tune up your senses to be aware of your surroundings, you will be astonished at how often you will spot opportunities to change your life for the better. An optimist is someone who believes this is true – not only because they have experienced it but because they know that this gives them the best chances in life.

Yes, things will go wrong for you from time to time. On average, it will be no more than for the next person. If you focus on your problems, however, it will always seem more, whether it is or not. An optimistic frame of mind will allow you to focus not on the problem, but on the aspects of your situation that you can actively manage.

Real optimists do not ignore risk; they embrace it. They identify risks, but instead of fearing them, they assess those risks realistically. Where the risks seem serious in terms of outcome or likelihood of occurring, they focus on how they can manage the risk, by reducing its impact, or making it less likely to occur. Or, at the very least, they think through how they can deal with the situation, should the risk manifest itself.

Choose the people you associate with

The last way to boost your optimism is to choose the people you associate with. If you habitually spend time with pessimists, you won't be able to help it: some of their attitudes will rub off. On the other hand, select optimistic colleagues, friends and contacts to spend more time with, and you will find it much easier to share their optimistic outlook.

This does not mean you have to abandon valued friends just because of their attitudes. What it does suggest is that, if you hear me moaning about how bad it is and that it will be bound to get worse, you will be better off finding an excuse to move on from the conversation: *'I'd like to think you're wrong and that we can find ways to thrive as things change around us. Let's agree to differ and talk about something else.'*

Determination, flexibility and persistence

We talked about the value of setting goals in Chapter 4. Resilient people are those who know their goals, understand their value, and take determined steps to achieve them. They also know how to cope with setbacks.

Determination

Determination is about having a measure of single-mindedness, without being blinkered to other opportunities or events. The behaviours that characterise it are planning and prioritisation, setting aside time and resources to pursue your goals, reviewing progress, and incorporating the lessons you learn along the way. If you are determined, you will see obstacles as challenges to overcome, and setbacks as temporary.

Flexibility

If two people experience the same setback, and they want the same thing, then the one who is more flexible in their thinking will usually find the solution first; the one who is most flexible in their behaviour will get what they want; and the one who is most flexible in their response to change will feel that they are in control. Flexibility is about creating choices and is what stops determination becoming obsession. To be flexible, you need to be able to step back from a challenge, see it objectively, and then find a wide range of options. The process to SCOPE a problem that you read in Chapter 5 will help you to step back, but sometimes you need more resources. Give yourself time, refresh yourself with a walk in the open air, consult friends or colleagues, or pick up some random books or magazines for stimulus.

Persistence

'If at first you don't succeed, try something else.'

We saw this in Chapter 3, but the key here is to keep trying. Once again, know the boundary between determination and obsession, but also know that failure is rarely inevitable.

Gratitude

Prayer has been a part of human life and public ritual for as long as recorded history. Only now are we finding out why it is so powerful in bringing about change and a sense of wellbeing. And it need not have anything to do with religion: if you have a faith, you can believe what you choose about how prayer works, and if you have none at all, you can reflect on what modern science is learning.

Maximisers and satisficers

The psychology of decision-making divides us neatly into two groups, the *maximisers* and the *satisficers*. Which are you?

- If you are a maximiser, you usually want the best product, solution or deal. You will examine every option very carefully and will agonise over details. Missing information can lead you to get stuck and not feel able to decide.

- If you are a satisficer, then you know what you want and will happily decide on the first product, solution or deal that meets your needs. 'Good enough' is good enough for you.

Not surprisingly, maximisers do better in life; they achieve more and get better stuff. But, and this is important, satisficers are happier. They feel better because they do not constantly worry that they didn't get the best; they are simply grateful for what they got, and move on. Maximisers, however, spend a lot of time regretting decisions that did not turn out to be optimal, and wanting ever more than they already have. This leads to a lot of wasted time and a lot of self-recrimination.

So, be grateful for what you have and avoid making comparisons with what other people have. You didn't need a bigger TV when you bought that one, so why do you need it now, just because Chris and Stevie bought one that's 15 cm bigger? Too much choice can stifle decision-making, so only consider a small number of options and don't expand your range, unless none of them meets your essential criteria.

Past positive

Some people focus on the here and now, and can lose themselves in the moment. Others focus on the future and what they can do tomorrow, so losing the joy of today. But the people who have the greatest sense of wellbeing are those who look back on their past with affection. They can see the mistakes and the pain, but do not dwell on it. They are grateful for everything that has come into their lives, learning from adversity and cherishing the pleasures.

brilliant exercise

Make a list of ten key events or moments in your past – good and bad.

For each one, spend a few minutes reflecting on what good things came out of it: what you enjoyed, what you learned, how it has made you better. Work hardest on the events that are most painful. What resources did they give you, what did you discover about yourself or the people around you? With the most joyous events, take a few minutes to savour the memories and make them even more a part of who you are now.

Being grateful

'*Polo: the mint with a hole.*' It is very easy to focus on what we don't have. Research shows that people feel better and make better decisions when they focus on what they have and when they feel a sense of gratitude for the good things in their lives.

If you make a habit of just taking a moment to be grateful when something goes well, you will start to boost your sense of well-being. To get a head start, take some time to jot down all of the things in your life that you can be grateful for. For example: family, friends, colleagues, sunshine, small successes, a favourite book or TV programme, your education, a kindness somebody did you, your health … The list could be endless.

When you feel really down and stressed out, there is an industrial-strength approach that certainly got me out of a hole when stressed by a combination of events: a move to a new home in a new area, the inevitable late nights of unpacking, shifting and cleaning, the birth of my daughter, the illness of a close relative, a heavy workload, and finally a slipped disc. If you want a fresh perspective on your life, you need a gratitude journal.

brilliant activity

Gratitude journal

Get yourself a fresh notebook and pen – nice ones are ideal – and on the first page write the date and the words 'Gratitude Journal'.

Each night, before bed (or maybe in bed before you turn out the light), write the date and write down what you feel grateful for there and then. It will often be for something that happened during the day. It can also be something bigger in your life that you are grateful for. You may write about one thing or several. You may write at length or briefly. You may write prose or just notes – you may even write verse. It does not matter what you write, as long as you write something.

Keep this up for at least a month, but feel free to keep going longer. Many people find it so valuable that it becomes a habit, and their gratitude journal becomes their form of daily journal. What you will notice is how different you start to feel about your life, as your troubles are set back into perspective among the many, once forgotten, things that you have to be grateful for.

Self-talk

Most of us say things to ourselves that we would never dare say to the people around us; things that would offend, demean and belittle. Are these the sorts of things you say to yourself when you feel under stress and things are not going your way? If so, this is strange, as it is the one conversation you have total control over.

This is important because a well-chosen word can give you a massive boost. Consider the difference between: *'I'm rubbish'* and *'That did not go well … this time.'*

A 24-hour motivation coach … for free

Now, if you could say motivating, empowering things, what would you say to yourself now? And you *can* say these things to yourself, can't you? Of course you can. Also think about how you say things. Consider the difference between: *'I got really lucky,'* which credits your success to luck, and *'I really grabbed that opportunity and made a huge success of it,'* which gives you the credit. Words are important. Start to notice the words you choose and make the choices that give you a real boost. They offer flattery, motivation, confidence building and a mental boost – all for free!

make yourself your own motivational coach

Make yourself your own motivational coach. Don't worry about being over-the-top and cheesy, because nobody can hear you. It's time someone loved and believed in you, and you can have their voice with you all the time, telling you that setbacks are temporary, problems are there to resolve, and your successes are triumphs. Whenever you do something good, or things go well for you, tell yourself: *'Well done'* or *'That was good.'*

Victim talk and survivor talk

We saw earlier in this chapter how important it is to take control of the meaning you attach to events. Events are what they are. What impacts upon us is the interpretation we put on them. You can control your sense of the meaning of events and how they affect you by choosing the questions you ask yourself. No longer see yourself as a victim: start to see yourself as a survivor. For example:

A victim will ask:	*'Why is life so unfair?'*
A survivor will ask:	*'What is really happening here?'*
A victim will ask:	*'Why will nobody listen to me?'*
A survivor will ask:	*'What is there that I can do?'*
A victim will ask:	*'Why me?'*
A survivor will ask:	*'What opportunities are there for me?'*
A victim will ask:	*'Whose fault is it?'*

A survivor will ask:	*'What can I learn from this?'*
A victim will ask:	*'When is it all going to end?'*
A survivor will ask:	*'Where do I want to be in six months?'*

The questions you ask dictate the answers you get. If you want good answers, you have to ask good questions.

Who are you?

One of the things we all do is put all sorts of labels on ourselves. Few are genuinely neutral with respect to our self-esteem and mental self-talk, because of the associations we attach to them. Some, however, can be genuinely destructive, while others can be life-enhancing. A lot of them arose early in our lives when we were too naïve to question them.

'I'm an idiot.'
'I'm clumsy.'
'I'm born unlucky.'
'I'm uneducated.'
'I'm a failure.'

You must get rid of these labels and any like them. Instead, replace them with honest labels that describe the best in you; and use positive adjectives too. If you value your role as a husband or wife, then *'I'm a husband'* or *'I'm a wife.'* But go further: *'I'm a husband who does everything he can to be a good one'* or *'I'm a wife who loves my husband.'* If you value learning but had little education: *'I'm someone who will take any opportunity to learn something new'* or, if you once knocked over the crockery at a department store, how about: *'I'm someone who makes an effort to be aware of what's around me'*?

Be good to yourself

In everything you say to yourself, treat yourself well; treat yourself like royalty. You would never raise your voice to a queen or a president, so don't do it to yourself. Change the tone of the voice, so that it is steady, friendly and authoritative. And be polite!

Breaking the cycle

So far, all of the attitudes and tools we have discussed have given you individual ways to improve your mental response to stress, but you may need a systematic way to regain total control. This final section offers you a powerful four-step process.

Step 1: Mature reflection

The basis of one of the most popular forms of therapy, CBT or Cognitive Behavioural Therapy, is Albert Ellis's ABC Model. This shows you the three components of a situation that you need to understand before you can gain control over it.

A: Activating event

… or Adversity; this is the objective event that causes you concern. Sometimes it is not clear, when you are stressed, what has triggered your emotions, so reflect on everything that has happened, and how you feel about it.

B: Beliefs

Next, examine the beliefs you have (rational or not) about the event, which set off your stress, fears and subsequent responses.

C: Consequences

Ultimately, what consequences do those beliefs have for you in terms of what you do and how that changes your options and opportunities?

Step 2: Honour your emotions

It is okay to feel emotions – they are a part of what makes us all human. You cannot control your stress unless you recognise those emotions and accept them as yours. The process of reviewing how you feel at times of stress, anger, grief or fear is the first step in defusing the emotions and robbing them of their power over you.

Step 3: Look for the evidence

Now you are ready to challenge your beliefs about yourself and your environment, and how they affect your interpretations of the events that triggered your stress. In Chapter 10, you will learn a whole host of ways to challenge them by focusing on the evidence you have been blind to: the evidence that contradicts your faulty thinking.

Step 4: Choose your behaviour

With your new perspectives, you are ready to start changing your behaviour. Start to seize control and do something different: control your physical responses to stress, control your environment, control your time, and control your attitudes

brilliant tip

If the stress cycle is too strong for you, you may not be able to do it on your own. Find someone to help you: an advisor, a coach, a mentor or a friend. Choose someone whose life is in balance, who has the time to listen and the wisdom to advise you well. If the stress cycle is too strong for them, choose a professional counsellor. Above all, find someone whom you trust – implicitly.

brilliant recap

- You get what you focus on, so, in times of stress, focus on your resources and your options, rather than on your troubles and constraints.

- Take an optimistic outlook, by being aware of what you want and scanning your environment for opportunities to move in the right direction.

- Knowing what you want, be prepared to work hard to get it, changing your approach if what you try does not work.

- Take stock of all the things that you can be grateful for. A gratitude journal is one of the best ways to see your way through your woes.

- Be your own motivational coach – tell yourself you are in control, give good advice, and congratulate yourself on every success.

CHAPTER 7

Manage stress at work

n 2009/10, the UK Health and Safety Executive (HSE) estimated that between 8 and 11 million working days were lost
to the UK economy due to stress. This was the largest single
cause of lost productivity. It has an economic cost of around
£1 billion and equates to 1.5 per cent of people who worked in
that year suffering from stress caused or made worse by work
at some time during those 12 months. Stress accounts for just
over 40 per cent of days lost to illness: it is a big workplace
issue.

And these figures are only the most obvious consequence
of stress. Others include increased staff turnover, with all of
the cost and disruption that causes, accidents, errors and
poor judgement, damage to workplace relationships among
colleagues and with customers, and simple reductions in
productivity.

This chapter therefore considers stress at work:

- How to spot it
- Managers' responsibilities
- How to reduce the stress you cause your colleagues,
  particularly if you are a manager
- How to support team members who show signs of stress
- Turning around a stressed work environment
- How to protect yourself from stress at work

Signs and portents

Stress in a workplace becomes visible in two ways: through changes in individuals, and through change across a team or across your entire staff. We'll examine the indicators for these one at a time. You may like to make a tally of how many you are aware of among your colleagues and in your workplace.

Individual signs of stress

It would be very rare for all of these signs to be present and, indeed, some will depend on the individual's personality. In fact, one of the commonest yet most subtle signs of stress is when personality traits and characteristics become more pronounced. Other things you may notice include:

Health

- Fatigue, tiredness
- Coughs, colds, recurrent illness
- Frequent headaches
- Back, neck and shoulder pain
- Twitching, tics (eye area particularly), hand tremors
- Stomach or bowel problems, indigestion, flatulence
- Skin disorders, greasy or spotty face, flare-ups of acne, eczema or psoriasis
- High heart and breathing rates – perspiration, flushing
- Weight loss/gain

Mood and emotional

- Tension, irritability, mood swings
- Anger and frustration
- Tearfulness, crying
- Anxiety, listlessness, depression
- Loss of motivation/commitment

- Oversensitivity to small things or under-sensitivity to major issues

Behavioural

- Poor concentration, indecision, forgetfulness
- Declining/inconsistent performance
- Uncharacteristic errors
- Lapses in memory
- Poor timekeeping, absences, leaving early
- Increased time at work
- Poor posture
- Appearance and personal care decline
- Nail biting, lip biting
- Stimulant abuse – coffee, cigarettes, alcohol
- Fidgeting, drumming fingers
- Door, drawer, phone slamming
- Arguments and conflict with colleagues, customers and other people
- Risk-taking and accidents

Collective signs of stress

Across a whole team or organisation, you may start to notice systemic trends from a rise in the incidence of undesirable indicators. These statistical features may only provide solid evidence after a long period, but if you are monitoring them frequently enough, they can provide early indicators that you need to be on the alert for personal signs of stress that you can deal with quickly.

- Increased absence levels
- Poor timekeeping
- General poor health

- Staff turnover increases
- Productivity falls
- Quality drops
- Complaints increase
- Gossip and rumours increase
- Bad atmosphere/low morale
- Poor relationships, disputes, conflict
- Dissension, insubordination, poor industrial relations
- Bullying
- Increased late working – with or without formal overtime
- Accidents and near misses

You *must* deal with it

If you have any managerial responsibility – whether as a front-line supervisor or all the way up to managing director or chief executive – you must deal with stress as soon as you are aware of it. If you are a member of staff, and are aware of stress in yourself or a colleague, then please do let your supervisor or manager know. You and your colleagues have a right to expect managers to deal effectively with workplace stress. In the next section, we'll overview a manager's responsibilities.

Your responsibility as a manager

Your general responsibility

Before we look at the legal situation, let's assess what your responsibilities are as a manager, and at what a good organisation can expect of the people it puts in charge of others.

Take stress seriously

Managers should consider the control of workplace stress as a part of their core role. Actively look out for opportunities to reduce stressors, and ways to give staff control over their workplace and work practices. Constantly scan trends and observe your colleagues for signs of stress. Act on any signs swiftly, showing staff that you are doing something positive, and engage them in designing solutions.

Treat staff fairly and consistently

Create a workplace where stressors are kept to a minimum and staff are able to deal with them effectively to control their own stress levels. Important features of this are two-way communication with your staff group, and with each individual, and looking for opportunities for flexibility in working conditions and timings, to allow staff members more personal control. Give staff the training and support they need and allow them to personalise their work space and to do things their own way (of course, complying with mandatory requirements and processes). Do not tolerate any forms of bullying or harassment from colleagues, customers or suppliers.

Think carefully about your own management practices

Examine the way you interact with staff to discover whether the way you do things increases or decreases stress levels around you. You may feel able to ask for feedback – either from staff or from trusted colleagues who can observe the way you deal with team members. Always be prepared to make changes.

The law

The law around the workplace is complex, different in each country, and beyond the scope of this book. However, in the UK and many countries, there is a mesh of principal legislation aimed at protecting people at work, general legislation that is relevant to people at work, and case law.

In the UK, the most important legislation is contained within the Health and Safety at Work Act 1974 and Management of Health and Safety at Work Regulations 1999, which set out employers' duties towards all employees, for their health, safety and welfare. If you are in the UK, the Health and Safety Executive (HSE) is an excellent first port of call for information, guidance and standards in this area, and, if you are not, their website may still be a valuable additional resource to those available in your country.

How much stress do you cause?

Stress is different from the normal buzz of a healthy workplace, where pressure to produce something or serve customers or clients creates tensions from time to time. However, sometimes the pressures can become excessive or continue for too long, and managers are often part of the problem. Do you cause stress for your colleagues and team members?

 brilliant activity

Assess your stress-causing behaviours

How many of these boxes can you tick? The more you tick, the greater the risk you are putting your colleagues under.

Fixed workplace stress factors – out of your immediate control

Score two points for each tick.

 New technology

☐ Changing workplace culture, leading to uncertainty and fear

☐ Economic pressures

☐ Bullying or harassment are present

☐ Workloads and deadlines are at a high level and have been for a while

Your own managerial behaviours

Score one point for each tick.

☐ You are moody – sometimes up and sometimes down.

☐ You have favourites and also people you don't much like – and let it show.

☐ You ask people to do things, then fail to follow up or thank them.

☐ People ask you to do things and you find yourself letting them down.

☐ You are always in a rush and ask for things at the last minute.

☐ You are particularly good at spotting mistakes and inefficiencies.

☐ You are particularly poor at congratulating people for good work.

☐ You are very competitive and want to succeed personally.

☐ You work very hard and expect others to do so too.

☐ You feel that people should put their work before their own needs while they are at work. ·

If you add up your points, you will get a score out of 20. If you scored five or more, stress is a risk; if 10 or more, you need to take action now. If you scored 15 or more, stress should be your number one priority: people could get hurt.

As we saw at the start of the chapter, stress at work is a major problem. Workers frequently report that the major sources of stress for them are:

● Excessive workload

● Feeling undervalued

● The type of work they have to do is not what they want or are trained for

● The pressure to meet deadlines

- Having to take on other people's work (to cover for absences, for example).

Other sources of stress

It may not all be down to you or your workplace. People bring stress with them to work from home, family and social lives. While these are usually the primary source of stressors, workplace stressors can often be the triggering factors to major physical or mental health problems. These sources of stress can be linked to crisis and trauma, problems with home life, personal problems, financial problems, or physical and health problems. In addition, certain life events are likely to trigger serious stress responses. These include pregnancy or birth, divorce or relationship breakdown, a death or family illness, family conflict, or financial loss and debt.

people bring stress with them to work from home, family and social lives

How to not impose stress

This section offers managers a series of useful ways to reduce your impact on overall stress levels of your staff. It is arranged under six headings, reflecting the six management standards developed by the UK Health and Safety Executive (HSE). These are well researched and you will find a lot of supporting information on the HSE's website.

Manage the demands on staff

The principal demand that an employer places on its staff is their workload and the working patterns that form it. However, there are others, like the physical environment it offers, the tools and equipment it provides and the managerial processes and styles to which staff are subjected.

Workload

As a manager, it is your responsibility to assess each person's work, their workload and their working hours to ensure that they are consistent with their training and with safe practices. Identify any potential harm and deal with it immediately. Continue to monitor and manage workloads and resolve issues as they arise. This means that wise managers will always have a contingency plan – a 'plan B' – that will allow them to step in with alternatives, and offer support where needed.

Physical environment

Beyond what should be obvious – that the physical environment should meet all health and safety at work criteria and be subject to a suitable risk assessment – part of your role as a manager is to act as a champion for your team and fight for the best possible tools and equipment, which will help them to do their work effectively and efficiently.

Managerial style

It isn't possible, in this small space, to fit a whole book on good management style, but three management behaviours are particularly relevant to minimising the stressors you impose on staff:

1 Motivate positively. Apply the carrot, not the stick, and offer appropriate recognition and rewards for good performance, rather than rely on threats, punishments or inducements.

2 Give effective feedback and constructive advice. Good feedback will help team members to develop their abilities and perform better. Base your feedback on observed behaviour and balance any recommended changes with credit for things they do well.

3 Think before you speak or act. Diving into a situation without fully assessing it or getting staff perspectives can be

one of the most stressful behaviours. Always take time to SCOPE the situation.

Give staff control over the way they work

A sense of control is essential to avoid stress, so what do too many organisations do? They remove all control over the working day from large numbers of staff. Yet it is these very staff who probably know best how they can improve their own efficiency, deliver better services or make improved products. Consult your team and listen to their ideas. Give them as much autonomy as you possibly can – which is probably a lot more than you think you can now. Let them plan their work patterns where possible and, where they cannot, sit down and plan their workload for them in a way that shows real consideration for them and their personal lives.

Provide support to staff

Three things people want from their managers are honesty, respect and understanding. Create a supportive culture where people feel able to ask for help and you have the time to give it. You need to be respectful of people's needs both in and outside work. Although you are not obliged to always act on needs arising from their personal lives, it is wise to take them into consideration and, where you can, accommodate them. This will make people more effective at work and build loyalty.

Talk about stress

Stress is a reality of work, so mature managers acknowledge this and build a dialogue about it into their day-to-day work. Keep your eyes and ears open for signs of stress, and identify who is vulnerable. Take decisive action to pre-empt serious consequences. Remember your remote workers on different sites or working from home.

Promote positive workplace relationships

Most of us spend more of our waking time with our work colleagues than we do with the people we choose to make a life with
– our family and closest friends. So, workplace relationships are
very important to people. Get to know each of your team members
personally and give time to each person. Appreciate their differences and accommodate them, as best you can, when making
choices about work allocation and development opportunities.
Promote effective and respectful workplace communication and
consider whether and how to use formal team-building activities
in addition to your day-to-day management.

Be clear about staff members' roles

People want to know what you expect of them. If they do not
have enough certainty about their role, they will lose confidence
in your leadership, leaving them fearful and subject to stress.
On the other hand, however, if you subject people to roles that
are too rigidly defined, that will be stressful too, because of the
lack of control. The only solution is to get to know each of your
team members well, so that you can get the balance just right
for each one.

Consult team members and listen
to their opinions and ideas, involve
them in planning roles and responsibilities, and keep them informed
of any changes. Review their devel-

> consult team members
> and listen to their
> opinions and ideas

opment needs regularly and act on what you learn. This whole
process must begin with clear job descriptions and person speci-
fications and a rigorous recruitment process, to ensure that the
people you recruit are well-suited for their jobs.

Change is unsettling, so manage it well

Change is such an important workplace stressor that we have
given over a whole chapter, Chapter 8, to the topic. Here,

then, are just four essential tips to avoid imposing unnecessary stressors.

1 Have a clear plan and communicate it relentlessly.

2 Show determination, but not inflexibility.

3 Expect resistance and engage with it positively.

4 Be respectful of staff and try to empathise with their concerns.

Supporting team members with stress

The last chapter in this book, Chapter 10, is about helping others to manage their stress, so this section will focus on specifically managerial and workplace approaches. Much of Chapter 10 will also be relevant.

It is also important at these times to review your management practices. Consider all of the ideas in the previous section and how you can further reduce the stressors you are applying to a vulnerable person.

Provide resources

The most important thing that you can do to help is to make it easy to ask for help. You may not be the best person to directly respond, but, if you are receptive to requests and are aware of the resources your organisation can offer, you will start to offer choices and control to the person who has come to you.

Just allowing someone to vent their frustration, anger or upset can be a huge help too. The next step is to look at what specific support you can give to alleviate particular stressors. Examples include generosity around hours and breaks, reducing the need for travel, or changes in the work assigned or the people to work with. The most important thing to ask is: '*What changes would help you the most?*' Don't try to second guess how people want to be helped. Some, for example, need to lose themselves in work to help deal with a stressful situation in their private lives, whilst others need a light workload to give them time to deal with it.

Beyond this, larger organisations and trades unions can offer a range of valuable support services and there are some contact details at the end of this chapter. Some of the resources that you may be able to point people towards (in the workplace context) are:

- Occupational health
- Mediation (you will find more on this in Chapter 9)
- Counselling (there is more on this in Chapter 10).

Turning around a stressed work environment

The Health and Safety Executive (HSE) has a helpful five-step process for assessing risk, which applies well to the risks arising from workplace stress.

Step 1   Identify the hazards.

Step 2   Decide who might be harmed and how.

Step 3   Evaluate the risk and take action.

Step 4   Record your findings; make a plan and stick to it.

Step 5   Monitor and review.

This section offers you four areas where you can take action at Step 3.

Set up systems and processes

This is the formal side of protecting your business and your people from stress. It involves policies and procedures to ensure a safe workplace, formal systems to identify and deal with stress-related problems, and creating clear role definitions and effective working, to minimise capability- and workload-related stress.

Safe workplace

If the legal requirements do not provide a sufficient 'push', then you may need to create a business case to demonstrate the benefits of proactive stress management processes and practices – and, indeed, the potential costs of not having these.

It need not be a lengthy process to produce a basic policy, thanks to all of the resources available from statutory organisations and professional bodies. So, put your efforts into a successful launch that can win hearts and minds over to the value of your new policy.

Systems to deal with stress

Developing the systems you need will only be the first stage. You must also invest in training managers and supervisors to follow the processes well. Your basic system will cover things like monitoring absences and reviewing other indicators of stress, so that you can identify who is vulnerable and take action.

Effective working

Review job roles and the capabilities of your staff to allocate jobs effectively and spot development needs. Over the medium term, ensure each role has a good job description and person specification. Developing a robust recruitment process that can attract and identify the best candidates is an important strategic objective, as is a welcoming induction process that prepares people well for their role.

Empower staff to make changes

We have already covered a lot of the things you can do under this heading, like giving the training and support that staff need – not least on health, stress and safety matters. Empowering staff to make changes to their workplace and how they do their work is possibly the most valuable and effective way to change a high-stress culture around. It will take courage for managers to cede some real control, but it is often the staff who know exactly what needs to be done.

Initiatives like these need to be led from the very top of the organisation to have the credibility they need, to succeed.

Actively find and resolve problems

Problem solving is a large area, but making it a part of a new culture requires three vital things:

1 Establish processes for data collection.

2 Use structured analysis to find and address root causes.

3 Bring together diverse teams to plan and carry out remedial actions.

Create a wellbeing culture

The gold standard for a non-stressing workplace is one with a 'wellbeing culture' where staff are encouraged to take care of themselves, and their employer provides the resources to support them. Corporate gyms and relaxation rooms, on-site counsellors and masseurs all seem like an indulgence. But in some environments the reduction in absences and illness, and the increase in productivity and customer service can bring bottom-line results that more than pay for the investment and running costs. This will require a business case.

You may not need to go quite so far, to maximise a sense of wellbeing by prioritising health, fitness and relaxation. Just creating opportunities for flexible working and offering shower facilities for people who want to ride or run to work, or exercise at lunchtime, are a big start. You may then be able to offer some social, exercise or therapeutic resources, or consider subsidising their costs or giving over some working time to social activities.

Protecting yourself from stress at work

What can you do to protect yourself from the stresses and strains of a managerial role? Let's look at three major stressors for a typical manager.

Responsibility

'Uneasy lies the head ...'

As a manager you do have responsibility, so finding someone to talk to with experience of what you are dealing with is an important way to protect yourself – giving you a chance to vent, and as a source of advice. Another valuable asset is humility: you will get things wrong, so do the best you can and accept your setbacks as chances to learn.

Too busy

Not only do you have your own work, but you need to be there for every member of your team too. Make sure you schedule time off to relax, and plan your work accordingly. Scheduling private thinking and planning time is a great tool that many managers value highly. Delegate and prioritise as much as you can, so you can focus on what matters most.

Not liked

Sometimes you won't be liked; you may be resented, despised, hated even. It may not be in your job description, but it sometimes goes with the job. Keep your attention on what matters most, do things properly and, above all, always do the right thing. If you can achieve that, you may not be liked, but people will respect you.

⌐ brilliant tool

Personal incident diary

If you find yourself getting stressed, start to keep a personal incident diary. At the end of each day, note any incidents that stressed you out. For each incident, answer seven questions:

1 What happened?
2 Who was involved?
3 How did you respond?
4 How did it turn out?
5 What did you learn?
6 What will you do next time?
7 What are you grateful for?

🡵 brilliant resources

- Advisory, Conciliation and Arbitration Service (ACAS):
  www.acas.org.uk/index.aspx?articleid=1993
- British Association for Counselling & Psychotherapy (BACP):
  www.bacp.co.uk
- The Chartered Institute of Personnel and Development (CIPD):
  www.cipd.co.uk/subjects/health/stress
- Health and Safety Executive (HSE): **www.hse.gov.uk/stress**
- Institute of Occupational Safety and Health (IOSH): **www.iosh.co.uk**
- Trades Union Congress (TUC): **www.tuc.org.uk**

⟳ brilliant recap

- Spot the health, mood and behavioural signs of stress in individuals, and the collective signs of stress across your whole team.
- You must take stress seriously and deal with it.
- Be aware that, as a manager, you may be causing some of the stress in your team. Look for ways to minimise this.

▶

- The right systems and processes can turn around a workplace environment, and there is a lot of help available from professional and statutory bodies.

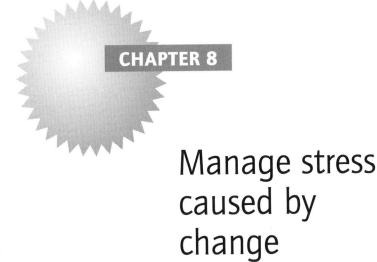

CHAPTER 8

Manage stress caused by change

External change is beyond our control, so it is no surprise that we find it stressful. Our ancient ancestors had to deal with quickly changing and often life-threatening situations, like the appearance of a large, hungry predator. However, once they had evaded capture, their sympathetic nervous system could calm down and the stress hormones dissipate. Now we find ourselves living with constant change and the uncertainty it produces. We need to find ways that, if we cannot control the change, we can still feel 'in control' of ourselves and our futures.

This chapter explains how change happens and how we respond to it, before looking at techniques you can use to cope in times of change. It ends with a way by which you can focus yourself on what you really want and so find opportunities to do more than just survive: in other words, to thrive in times of change.

How change happens in the world

Change often seems to creep up on you and catch you unawares. It has been happening quietly for a while, but it takes a seemingly random incident to bring it to your attention. For example, the paint and decorative finish of your home can be deteriorating slowly and imperceptibly for years, but it sometimes takes a visitor to notice it: *'Mike, the paint on this wall is starting to peel.'*

This creates a moment of insight when a light bulb goes on in your head and you think: *'Aha … Change.'*

So you start to investigate your options, looking at paint colours and checking your budget to see if you can afford a new carpet. You finally settle on a colour, buy some paint and get decorating. When you are finished, life seems just a little better; you are proud of your new living room, and you enjoy it. Of course, you start by keeping it immaculate, but gradually the novelty wears off and you are back to your old routine. Months pass and then years, and gradually the paintwork picks up some scuffs, and the carpet gets a few small stains, but you don't notice these, day to day.

Your living room looks the same in the morning as it did when you went to bed, and it looks the same in the evening as it did when you went out in the morning. So it comes as a surprise when, six years later, a cheeky visitor says: *'Mike, this carpet is a bit of a mess.'*

This familiar story already starts to show us why we so often find change stressful. For most of us, the first point at which we become aware that change is happening is when it is too late to stop it, and our only option is to react to it.

The example is a very low-impact one, but think about the changes in your workplace or in society as a whole. They all follow the same cycle, illustrated in Figure 8.1, below.

In any situation, your awareness of the change starts with the seemingly random incident. It is not truly random, because it is inevitable that you will become aware of the external change at some point, but often it strikes you as coming out of the blue – randomly. This triggers a cascade of emotional and reasoned responses that we shall explore in the next section, and it is only when you take action, and therefore seize control of the situation, that you will feel comfortable with your emotions.

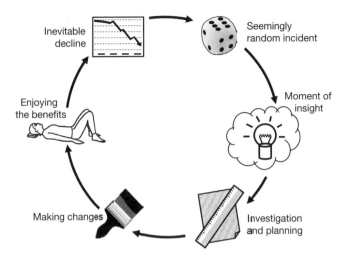

Figure 8.1 The change cycle

How you are programmed to respond to change

Figure 8.2 illustrates the emotional rollercoaster we all go through when faced with imposed change that we perceive as uncomfortable or threatening.

The rollercoaster of change

The curve in Figure 8.2 represents everyone's experience of change. What will differ – in often quite surprising ways – will be the nature and intensity of the emotions different people will feel, how they express them, and the pace at which they pass through the stages. Consequently, two people may experience the same situation quite differently and therefore feel quite different levels of stress. Let's look at each stage in turn.

Stage 1: Denial

Our first response to first realising that change is happening is usually denial. Our brains reject its discomforts and pretend it

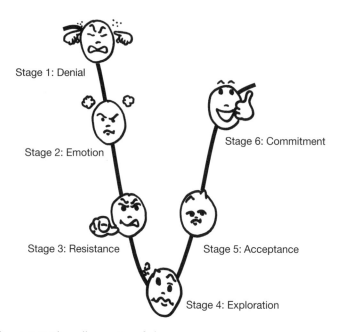

Figure 8.2 The rollercoaster of change

is not happening: before fight or flight comes fright. How often have you found yourself saying '*It will never happen*' or '*It won't affect me*' when, in your heart of hearts, you know it will? In front of others, we often dress it up as cynicism or scepticism, but we are really sticking our head in the sand and hoping it will go away.

Stage 2: Emotion

When we can no longer deny the reality of change, our emotional centres are the first to react. Depending upon how we perceive the change, our emotions can be strong or mild and of many sorts, from sadness to grief, frustration to anger, bitterness to disgust. They are a perfectly natural sign that the limbic system of our brain is engaged, and looking for ways to protect us, by triggering our fight-or-flight mechanisms.

There may also be a sense of relief and some positive emotions. Here, however, we are focusing on changes that are *perceived* as adverse or threatening – even if they are not really so.

When people start to get angry or upset about change, the last thing you should do is try to reason with them: '*There's no point in getting angry. Calm down and look at it rationally.*' This will just make them more angry or upset. Instead, you must respect their emotions and give them time to express them. The best thing you can do is to listen to them uncritically.

Stage 3: Resistance

Eventually, the power of our emotions subsides and they are replaced by reason. We start to become rational and start to think through the situation. We first tend to see the drawbacks associated with the change, because we focus on what we are losing, so this stage is characterised by a reasoned resistance to change. If you are trying to promote the change, then encountering this resistance is daunting, because there will almost certainly be pros and cons to the change, and now you have to deal with rational opposition.

The good news is that rational thinking allows us to analyse a situation and start to regain control. This stage is where we can start to fight the stress.

> rational thinking allows us to analyse a situation and start to regain control

Stage 4: Exploration

Once we are thinking in a rational way, we can start to evaluate the benefits as well as costs of the change. This stage is often the least energetic one, where we may feel frozen by inaction and with minimum control. But it is the stage where we explore our options and assess how to respond to the change. This choice can give us control, and, when we make our decision, we can seize control.

Stage 5: Acceptance

Having made our choice consciously, the next stage is where it sinks in, and we start to accept our new future. At the same time we also take our first steps to control our situation.

Stage 6: Commitment

The last stage of change is when we are fully committed to making changes and are in control. This does not mean that we like the change that has happened, but it does mean that we have completely accepted that we cannot change it and are therefore pursuing the next stage of our life.

A couple of examples

Let's look at two very different examples: someone who has suffered a bereavement, and someone whose employer changes the way that they operate at work.

A bereavement

Often people's first response to hearing of a loss is to say '*No, it can't be.*' We want to wind the clock back and make things different. This is denial. It is followed by a period of almost pure emotion: grief. The next stage sees people rage against the change, starting to consider the effects on them, their family and their plans. This is a form of resistance, which is followed by a quiet period of starting to come to terms with their loss. This turns into acceptance, when we fully realise that the loss is permanent. Only later do we start to move on with our lives and make a commitment to a new life without the person we have lost.

Without the acceptance and commitment, we cannot stop grieving and the bereavement has triggered a long-term problem.

A change at work

'*They've been talking about this for years. It will never happen. They wouldn't dare*' eventually becomes '*How dare they, good grief, oh no.*' We put off facing the inevitable change until we are confronted by it and then find ourselves getting angry with our bosses or upset, or bitter. At the root of all these emotions is the big one: fear. We fear the unknown, we fear not being able to cope, we fear failure. As the emotions subside, we find a dozen reasons why it won't work and resist the change, until we start to see how it could work – or is already beginning to work – and we then begin to explore what the change means to us. We come to accept that there is a new reality and eventually make a commitment to it.

If we cannot accept the change and commit to a positive future for ourselves, we cannot regain control, and we are lost.

Personal tolerance for change

Nobody likes change. On the other hand, we all embrace change all of the time.

The difference is the degree of change that will push each of us into discomfort. For some, that level of change is vast and, for others, even the smallest change is painfully unsettling. Existing stress will diminish your ability to cope with change, making what would otherwise seem like a minor tremor feel like a huge earthquake in your life.

How to cope with the stress of change

Because stress comes from a feeling of not being in control, the early stages of change are the hardest to cope with. You become suddenly aware that events are beyond your control, and then your brain hijacks your conscious control and floods your being with emotion.

Your emotional response

So, to immediately start to regain control, make a conscious choice to respect your emotions. Your emotional cycle is natural and overpowering, so accepting it is the only real control you can have over it. And while you are at it, look around you: you are not alone. Respect other people's emotions too.

The way to move on from a highly emotional state is to examine your emotions. Ask yourself:

'Exactly what emotions am I feeling?'

'What is causing these emotions?'

'What am I afraid of?'

In examining your emotions in this way, you are being respectful of them, but starting to discharge them and move your brain into a more rational mode. Now is the time to take control of your health. If you are to respond resourcefully to difficult changes, you need to be as rested, fit and well fed as you can, so make a conscious decision to prioritise eating well, exercising and getting enough sleep or good-quality rest.

Your rational response

Now that your brain is in a reasoning mode, you will start to recognise all of the threats and challenges ahead. To avoid becoming paralysed by fear, share your concerns with somebody else. There is a lot of emotional truth in the old saying that *'a problem shared is a problem halved'*. With someone whom you trust that you can speak to, you can express your resistance and start to explore your options without feeling too exposed to the wide world when you do it.

> to avoid becoming paralysed by fear, share your concerns with somebody else

The most important thing you can do in seizing control is to base your choices on the best available evidence. So, ask questions and find out the facts. Separate truth from rumour, invite different points of view and, in particular, listen to positive perspectives. You do not want to miss some good news while focusing on the bad. This requires you to keep an open mind about how the change can benefit you.

Your anchors

In the tides of change, it is valuable to review your anchors – the things that hold you down. Set aside a little time to review who you are and what is most important in your life. The exercise below will give you a structured way to do this.

brilliant exercise

Your anchors

Write down these questions and your answers to them. If you have a gratitude journal (see Chapter 6), this would be a good place to record this.

Who has influenced the way you are?

… and what did they teach you?

Who is most important to you in life?

… and what do you value them for?

What is most precious to you in life?

… and what do you cherish about it?

What are you most grateful for?

… and what is really worth fighting for?

Your attitudes

Three attitudes that featured in Chapter 6 are of particular significance in coping with major change: optimism, flexibility and gratitude. Optimism will help you prime yourself to spot opportunities that arise, and times of change are times when opportunities come in abundance. Flexibility will allow you to adapt to the changing circumstances and to seize opportunities quickly, even when they come in an unexpected form or from an unexpected place. Gratitude will help you to focus on what is good in your situation, rather than dwelling on what you may lose, on how tough things are, or on your fears.

Put simply, what theme song are you going to choose for yourself? Will you choose the Rolling Stones' 'It's all over now', or will you choose Gloria Gaynor's 'I will survive'? If you choose 'I will survive', these three winning attitudes are proven to give you an advantage.

Your actions

Nothing gives you more control than getting involved. Look for ways that you can help to drive the change agenda and influence outcomes. It is very easy to get stuck in a rut and spend your time with other miserable people bemoaning how you are all victims of the change. But this is an important final point of control: choosing the people you associate with. Do you associate with 'victims' or 'survivors'?

It's not just your attitude that counts; it's the attitudes of the people around you. Even the strongest willed among us find it hard to stay optimistic in the teeth of unrelenting pessimism. It is human nature to want to join in. So, make it easy for yourself by joining people who have a positive attitude too. Build powerful working relationships with the people who can support you and help you to not just survive, but to thrive. This will help you to avoid indulging in the 'terrible trio' of rumours, rants and recriminations, which so often characterise responses to change.

Your pace of change

Uncomfortable as it may seem to you, the final piece of advice is to start adapting quickly. Rather like a trip to the dentist, most of the pain comes from the transition, not the end point. The sooner you start and the faster you move, the sooner you will start to feel comfortable again …

… until the next change comes along.

Final tips

At times of change, we often don't think very clearly about how to look after ourselves. At the back of this book is a quick list of 101 ways to reduce your stress. From time to time, dip into this list and try one out.

Dealing with personal loss or tragedy

Grieving is our natural response to a personal loss, and the closer the loved one was to us, the more intensely we will feel the pain of grief. This can often be exacerbated by circumstances. The loss of an elderly parent to natural causes, after a long and happy life, is part of the natural order, and very different from losing someone in their prime, or younger.

There are no fixed ways to grieve, and we all do it in our own way, mostly within a set of cultural norms. However, if you are dealing with a loss, or know someone who is, here are a few simple ways to help.

Don't ignore the pain
The pain of loss will not go away faster if you ignore it, but you may find that getting on with other aspects of your life is the way that you can cope best. It is okay to ask for help and to cry, but it is also okay not to do these things.

Finding support can help
Practical support is important, and if you can find someone to take care of the small details of life that will help you stay healthy, this will free you up to focus on your loss and deal with it in your own way.

Expressing your feelings

Someone who will listen can be a big comfort to many of us, but you may not find talking about your loss comfortable. Instead, you may prefer to write your thoughts down. Sometimes a letter to the person you have lost can help and, sometimes, just writing a few words about them. One of the reasons many cultures include a description of the departed in their rites is because formulating it can help us to grieve.

Expressing your faith

If you have a faith, you may find that its rituals or your relationship with your god are a source of comfort that help you to cope. Prayer can be a good way of talking about your feelings without having to find a person to listen.

Therapeutic support

Counsellors, religious ministers and support groups are readily available in most communities and can be a big support. The only caution is to be aware how easy it is to become dependent upon them for your emotional strength. Those who are skilled will be aware of this too.

More than survival

Whatever the change, you will eventually come out the other side. So, how can you do more than just survive? How can you thrive? Here is a four-step process that will show you how.

Step 1: Analyse

Examine carefully what resources you have. Identify your skills and experience, personality and knowledge, friends and colleagues. These will help you. Focus on the things that are most important to you. Take an inventory of what you have that can help you survive, develop and thrive.

Step 2: Aim

Think about what you want. Here, it is important to be careful to avoid the trap of wanting what you feel you ought to want, or worse, what other people expect you to want. Instead, think about what you really want. Be true to yourself and ask the question: *'What would I do if I knew I really could not fail?'*

When you have this, it will be massively motivating, so use that energy to think about how you are going to achieve it. The two things to focus on are these:

1 **What are the important steps along the way?**
   Identify milestones, waypoints, achievements, and markers of progress. This is important because these are your opportunities for success. And when you achieve successes, you can celebrate them. And when you celebrate, you feel good about yourself, so you increase in confidence. This leads to better performance and more success. More success: more celebrations. And so on up and up.

2 **What is the first step along the way?**
   This is important to get you started. Taking control of your change is a big thing. Taking one step is easy. And once you've taken one step, the second is easy ... And so on. As the Chinese proverb says: *'A journey of a thousand miles starts with a single step.'*

Step 3: Antenna

Once you know what you want, you have to tune your mental antenna to spot opportunities to get it. This is a tiny part of your brain, called the reticular activating system, which could better be called your 'serendipity organ'. Once you know what you are looking for, it is responsible for spotting things in your environment that conform to the pattern, and bringing them to your conscious attention.

It is like a hole in a toddler's toy. You programme it to a particular shape you are looking for, it examines everything you see, and finds the right peg to fit in the hole. You really can get what you look for in life.

Step 4: Action

You'll create no change without action, so get started as soon as you can. The most motivating feeling is when we know we have taken action and we can see the results. Taking action gives you a feeling of control; seeing the results will give you a feeling of succeeding.

Close the loop

Success comes from persistence, so close the loop. What you repeat becomes habit and it is your habits that determine the results you get in life. So, look at the outcome of your action and analyse your situation objectively. Review what you want and adjust your aim, retune your antenna to look for more opportunities, and take more action. Keep this up and you can have whatever success means to you.

This is more than just survival; this is thriving in times of change.

brilliant recap

- Change is inevitable and our response to it is a natural consequence of how we have evolved.

- We cope best with change by understanding our natural responses and working with them.

- Choosing the right attitudes will help you cope, as will getting involved and becoming proactive, which will restore a sense of control over events.

- Use the four-step process of Analyse – Aim – Antenna – Action to turn change to your advantage.

CHAPTER 9

Manage stress caused by conflict

onflict and stress feed one another. When you are more stressed, you are more likely to find yourself in conflict with the people around you, because your perspective on issues is not as clear as it could be. When you fall into conflict with others, it increases your stress levels. How to resolve conflict is an essential part of stress control.

Notice the phrase: *'when you fall into conflict'*. This is what it is often like: it seems as if you have reached the edge of the cliff and then ... you fall. Sometimes we know it is happening and feel unable to stop ourselves leaning over. This is often a sign of stress, so this chapter begins with how to recognise escalating conflict.

At the core of the chapter are two sections: five approaches to dealing with conflict, and a seven-step process for resolving conflict. The last section introduces two 'industrial-strength' solutions: mediation and arbitration.

How to recognise escalating conflict

Conflict has a way of escalating out of control. It all starts when harmony is disturbed by a simple irritant – usually something that is objectively very minor. Yet, to one party, it is significant and a failure to accommodate it leads to escalation.

As we meet resistance, we become annoyed then exasperated, moving to anger and maybe even rage. Conflict reaches its peak at various forms of abuse from verbal to physical violence, and it can all happen astonishingly quickly. Like stress, the later stages of this escalation are marked by a loss of control.

The warning signs

Therefore, if you can spot the signs early, it will help you to defuse the conflict while it is still relatively easy to do so. The essential skills are to observe behaviours and to listen carefully, particularly to the unspoken messages. Here are some of the warning signs that you can pick up from body language:

Discomfort

The first thing you might notice if you are observing two people is one or both of them shifting their posture from leaning in towards the other (accord) or a neutral posture, to leaning away from one another. This is an attempt to increase the space between them, signalling that they feel uncomfortable with that person.

As they start feeling insecure about their position, a telltale sign is neck touching. We do this to relieve insecurity, doubt or uncomfortable emotions, so you may see a man adjust his collar or tie, or a woman play with a necklace.

Disagreement

Annoyance is often signalled by short repetitive movements, such as tapping fingers or shifting weight from one foot to another. Both of these, however, could also indicate impatience, which may be positive: a keenness to proceed. So, also look out for distinct signs of disagreement. Frowning is often first, showing a struggle to understand either what is being said or why it is being said. This latter reason suggests disagreement and a stronger indicator will be when they raise their hand towards the eye. If the brow cannot cover enough of the eye, this gesture now truly strengthens the signal to disbelief or disagreement. We literally don't want to see what we are hearing.

Stress

A furrowed brow is a clear sign of anxiety or even stress, and if you see them rub their brow, they are struggling to process an idea. If the anxiety grows, you are likely to see self-comforting behaviours, like wrapping of the arms around the body or rubbing their hands on their thighs.

You will start to hear changes in the voice at this stage too. It will be faster, more breathy, and sentences will become more staccato in the way they are delivered. Body movements may mirror this and also become more jerky.

Anger

To spot anger, look for signs that the fight-or-flight reaction is engaged – faster breathing, pallid look and an increase in muscle tension. This last one is easiest to see around the jaw line, particularly in men. At the extreme, you may also see fists tighten and hear the pitch of the voice increase, as throat muscles tighten. In men, you will often hear instead a deliberate attempt to control their voice and lower the pitch to make them sound bigger and more powerful, and this will usually come with an increase in volume.

Dominance and submission

Watch hands. We use these both consciously and unconsciously to signal our status and attitude in a negotiation or conflict. If I point my finger or stab my hand in your direction, I am blaming you. If my palms are back and I stand or sit with the backs of my hands towards you, I feel dominant and I may try to assert my control with a two-handed, palms-down gesture, pushing my hands gently downwards from chest to waist height: '*Calm down*.' But, if I raise my hands, with palms towards you, I am submitting, '*Stop!*' If I hold my hands out, palms-up, I am being placatory without submitting: '*Trust me*.'

A word of warning

Please do not try to over-interpret a single gesture. Look for patterns and clusters of signs. A single gesture usually means nothing: I may touch my brow because I disagree, or maybe because I have an itch. I may hug my arms around my body because I am anxious, or because I am cold.

Recognising avoidance

Conflicts tend to escalate when people avoid contentious issues that need to get resolved, so the stakes have increased by the time we confront them. So, you know that there is a problem, but you don't address it and, despite your hopes, it does not go away. If you don't discuss it, the distrust and negative feelings towards the other person increase, as you start to fantasise about their motives and intentions, which is all you can do in the absence of real information.

This causes you to lose perspective on the real issue and start to attach blame for the situation. You hear yourself talk about the other person in abstract terms and with sweeping generalisations. They have ceased to be Jack or Jackie and are now he or she, who is '*always* this' and '*never* that'. So the tensions grow and the conflict escalates, even if the issue itself has not developed or grown in any way. Familiar?

Five approaches to dealing with conflict

We have five fundamental approaches to dealing with conflict.

Approach 1: Step away

Of course, avoiding conflict is sometimes the right thing to do. Step away when you cannot possibly win, when the issue really is not important, or if the emotional temperature is too high, and you want to wait for a better time to engage with another approach.

But do not use this as a tactic merely to put off the inevitable, or to goad the other person. Both will probably have the effect of escalating the conflict to no benefit for either party.

Approach 2: Make concessions

Making concessions to the other person is a way of de-escalating the conflict, but beware that each concession may encourage manipulative behaviour that seeks a further concession. So, make each new concession smaller than the last – about half of the value. This creates a self-limiting process. This is a good strategy when you realise that 'winning' on this issue is less important than maintaining good relations and can also sometimes set up a sense of obligation that can mean you will win concessions 'next time'. If there can be no next time, then this approach has less value.

If you find yourself using this approach a lot, check with yourself that it is fully justified each time, and not a sign of low self-esteem. Making concessions can be a passive behaviour, where you do not expect the concession to be reciprocated. Then it becomes appeasement.

Approach 3: Play to win

When the outcome really matters to you and you have no qualms about the risk of further escalation, then playing to win will be your preferred approach. Use this strategy when you know you are right and when there is no time for debate, or when there is no chance of defusing the conflict, and getting a resolution quickly will minimise the harm.

But avoid the cycle of aggressive or bullying behaviour when winning becomes an end in itself, and you do not consider the consequences of the approach, nor the rights and wrongs of the outcomes you are pressing for. This will lose you respect as well as friends, and will ultimately fail when you come up against someone bigger and stronger than you are.

Approach 4: Some give and take

'*I'll give up something, if you give up something too*' is a good solution if you need to defuse tension and work towards an acceptable compromise. It will not leave either party truly happy, as they survey what they have given up, but neither will it leave them seriously aggrieved if the parties have behaved fairly. Whilst Approach 2 is about making unilateral concessions, here they are balanced, and this approach should satisfy both parties' needs for a sense of equity. It is broadly cooperative and can get to a final position relatively quickly, once each is in the mood to concede.

Don't get too hooked on this approach or it will become a game that you play – setting up bargains and doing deals. If this happens, you will associate victory with getting a result, rather than with getting a good result. This is the equivalent, for negotiators, of selling at a loss.

Approach 5: Go for 'win-win'

> the gold standard for conflict resolution is a result where both parties feel they have won

The gold standard for conflict resolution is a result where both parties feel they have won, and got everything they wanted – and more. Instead of trading concessions as you do in Approach 4, here you are looking to add new things to the discussion to create advantages for each other. This is a time-consuming tactic that takes hard work and commitment, but the rewards can be huge in building up trust and respect.

Use this approach when the outcome is very important, and so is an excellent long-term relationship. It means investing in understanding each other and working together collaboratively. There may well be setbacks along the way and you may seek outside help in the form of a mediator, to support the process.

Seven-step process for resolving conflict

De-escalation starts with a commitment to respect the other person, and then working to build an understanding of them and their needs. You will need to work together to clarify each other's issues and positions, and separate them from your genuine needs, so that you can then start to explore possible solutions. When you choose one solution, you have the basis for a resolution and you can create a plan to move forward. This section gives a seven-step process for resolving conflict.

Step 1: Make the choice to engage positively

The first step is to acknowledge for yourself that conflict exists and decide that you will respect the other person. In your mind, separate the person from the problem – their behaviour might be appalling, but respect them even if you cannot respect how they handle themself.

In the SCOPE process (Chapter 5), this step corresponds to Stop.

Step 2: Make contact

Contact the other person and declare the breakdown in good communication and state your commitment to a process of resolving the dispute. Seek their commitment in return. Recognise that it may be hard for each of you, but offer your willingness to enter the process with an open mind.

Step 3: Appreciate the courage that the other party is showing

Be prepared to listen first and encourage honesty by respecting that whatever you hear, no matter how uncomfortable, it is what the other person thinks and feels. You may not agree, but it is their truth, so respect it. Demonstrate empathy for their feelings and show that you are prepared to work hard to understand their position.

Step 4: Understand each other's points of view

'Seek first to understand; then to be understood.'

Stephen Covey

Start to build rapport by listening hard (*'Listen more than you speak'* is a good rule) and look for common ground – issues and parts of issues that you both agree on. Share facts, feelings, perspectives, concerns and definitions, so that you can distinguish facts from opinions, and issues from positions. When you truly understand the other person's point of view, you may realise you have been wrong. If so, admit it straight away, apologise, and move on. Put progress in resolving the conflict ahead of your pride.

In the SCOPE process, this step corresponds to Clarify.

At this stage, you may find that the other person does not wish to resolve the conflict. It takes two to tango, so if this is the case, your only option is to make clear your desire to resolve things constructively, then courteously withdraw.

Step 5: Agree criteria for a resolution

What are your respective absolute requirements for a solution and what external pressures and time constraints are you both subject to? Use these to figure out and share your bottom-line criteria and, if they are wholly incompatible, you may agree that resolution is impossible and look for a way to coexist, without coming into conflict: a form of strategic avoidance.

When you have agreed your criteria, use them as a basis to reiterate your respective commitments to what you are now committed to do.

Step 6: Explore options and possible solutions

The two things to discover are:

- What is available to you both?
- What is missing?

Think of each of these in terms of resources, possibilities and processes. These will help you to identify your options.

Be creative and generate as many options as you can, by being flexible and taking ideas from all available sources. Be generous in crediting the other person with ideas. This will build trust and strengthen their commitment to the idea. Resolving the conflict should be more important to you than taking credit for how it happens.

In the SCOPE process, this step corresponds to Options.

Step 7: Offer a resolution

The last step is to agree on the best solution and then work together to plan your next actions. This stage will often include requests of – and promises to – each other, and these can solidify your sense of agreement and collaboration. It is always nice to mark the agreement in some way: maybe not formally, but informally, with either a statement that you have resolved the conflict and reached agreement, or perhaps a handshake.

In the SCOPE process, this step corresponds to Proceed.

Mediation and arbitration

When a conflict or dispute is too difficult for the disputants to resolve alone, two options for help are mediation and arbitration.

Mediation: an impartial person helps two or more people reach a solution that is acceptable to everyone.

Arbitration: an impartial person is asked to make a decision on a dispute.

In the UK, ACAS (Advisory, Conciliation and Arbitration Service) is a non-departmental body, funded by government to *'improve organisations and working life through better employment relations'*. They provide services to business and their website, **www.acas.org.uk**, offers a wealth of valuable information. There are also professional mediators and arbitrators who specialise in the whole range of personal and commercial issues.

Mediation

Workplace disputes can poison the atmosphere, leaving everyone miserable – not just the protagonists. You will want to resolve the situation as quickly as possible: before the words 'tribunal' or 'solicitor' are uttered, and here mediation can help. A mediator can often broker a resolution that both parties will agree to. For small disputes, some common sense and patience can help people find sufficient common ground to bury the hatchet. If you choose to help, then here is a basic process. Different mediators and different contexts mean that there is a range of variations on this theme.

> a mediator can often broker a resolution that both parties will agree to

A mediation process

Let's introduce the two people in conflict as Person A, the person who has declared the grievance, and Person B.

Step 1: Meet the first person (usually A) and listen carefully to their point of view and then confirm with A that they are prepared to meet B.

Step 2: Now meet B. Sometimes, this meeting starts with an agreement to pursue mediation; at other times, that agreement will already have been given. Listen carefully to their point of view, and then confirm with B that they are prepared to meet A.

Assuming both people have agreed to meet, you will need to reflect on what the fundamental issues are, before...

Step 3: Meet A to share information and plan a three-way meeting.

Step 4: Meet B to share information and plan a three-way meeting.

Step 5: Facilitate a meeting between A and B, at which they each listen to the other as they express their point of view. Ensure that all issues are shared and that each is listened to with care. Now help A and B explore their issues, and start to create an agreement.

Step 6: When A and B reach an agreement, you may not like it, but document it and ask A and B for formal confirmation with signatures or handshakes. You may even choose to formally witness it.

Step 7: In many cases, you will agree a follow-up role, to monitor how the agreement is working.

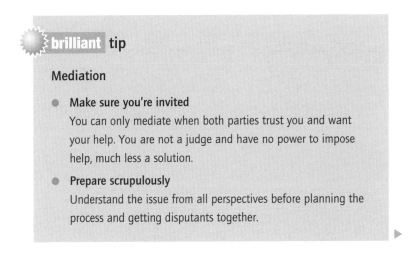

brilliant tip

Mediation

- **Make sure you're invited**
  You can only mediate when both parties trust you and want your help. You are not a judge and have no power to impose help, much less a solution.

- **Prepare scrupulously**
  Understand the issue from all perspectives before planning the process and getting disputants together.

▶

- **Create a safe environment and the time you all need**
  Disputes often persist because they are 'public property'. A confidential environment can help people express themselves honestly, and listen carefully.

- **Allow everyone to be heard**
  Your role is to create a process that ensures all are treated fairly. Let everyone be heard.

- **Find common ground**
  Listen, clarify and highlight areas of shared commitment. Help them narrow the area of disagreement.

- **Remain neutral**
  Once you hear the first perspective, it is natural to sympathise with that point of view. Who is 'right' is irrelevant here (and probably a false concept).

- **Above all, do no harm**
  If you are in any doubt about your ability to help, or the risk is too high, seek expert help.

Arbitration

It is unlikely that you will act as an arbitrator among colleagues you know, because they may not fully trust your impartiality. You may, however, arbitrate on a conflict in an area of your organisation about which you can be – and be seen by all to be – wholly impartial. If this is the case, then the process is similar to mediation, but you will make the final decision and may have the authority to impose it.

You will therefore need to be alert to any inadvertent biases that the process or the personalities of the protagonists can throw up. Below is a list of *brilliant do's and don'ts*.

brilliant do's and don'ts

Arbitration

Do

✔ Recognise that there will be merit on both sides or the issue would not need arbitration.

✔ Give the disputants a chance to rant if they want to.

✔ Put aside any temptation to help one party get even with the other.

✔ Separate facts from opinions.

✔ Ask more questions if you need to.

✔ Document everything.

✔ Maintain confidentiality.

✔ Test out your reasoning before giving your opinion.

Don't

✘ Assume that a poorly presented case is a poor case.

✘ Allow yourself to accept the first perspective you hear uncritically.

✘ Appear to take sides until you are ready with a considered opinion.

✘ Let the strength of emotions weight your considerations.

ACAS or other impartial organisations have trained personnel who can apply a transparent process and come up with a fair outcome, and using them can offer the only resolution to long-running conflicts, where cooperation is impossible and mediation has failed.

brilliant recap

● Look for the warning signs of escalating conflict, so you can defuse it early.

- There are five approaches to resolving conflict: choose the one that is appropriate to each situation.

- Follow a simple seven-step process to resolve conflict and, if this fails, consider using mediation or arbitration.

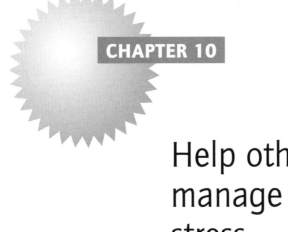

CHAPTER 10

Help others to manage their stress

At various points in *Brilliant Stress Management*, I have given you the advice to seek out help and support. This final chapter offers you some advice for when somebody comes to you for help and support. Having got this far in the book, you will already have a lot of resources, so this chapter is not about what advice to offer. Instead, it is about how to give your help and support effectively.

There are three sections in this chapter, which take you through advancing understanding of how to help, starting with listening well, then helping someone to regain control, and thirdly looking at one psychological model that will help you understand their need to apportion blame and how you can introduce reason into their thinking. Finally, because there is a limit to what you can achieve with goodwill and a few hours of reading, there is a list of resources at the end of the chapter, which sets out some of the places you can point them to for professional or highly experienced help, some of which specialise in particular life problems that result in stress.

Listening

The most valuable gift you can give someone who is struggling with stress is your total attention. There are three reasons: because we all want to be listened to, because it is important to let someone whose mind is in turmoil talk, and because you will be modelling the very opposite of what they are feeling – the ability to make a choice to do nothing but give your time to one very important thing. This can have a powerfully calming effect.

Making time

When somebody comes to you for help, it is a hard and uncomfortable thing they have done, so the most important response you can give is to be wholly respectful of this, and take it seriously. Even if you think that all is well, if, in their mind it is not, then it is not.

Look for an opportunity to listen to them, in a suitable place. The sooner the better; but it needs to be at a time when you can give them all of your attention. If they have caught you at a bad time then it is better to agree another time than to take time out and be stressed about this yourself. They will sense your stress and it will enhance theirs.

First response

It is tempting to say that your first response when you settle down to listen should be nothing. It is certainly true that you will need to work hard to suppress most of your reactions to what you hear: the temptation to probe, to judge, to give advice, to offer opinions, challenge or criticise, or even to tell your own story. None of these will help. Instead, your first response must be to show that you hear them and understand them.

Empathy is an understanding of another person's feelings, and maybe starting to 'feel for them'. We can do this because of a set of brain cells called 'mirror neurons' whose role is to spot movement, gesture and expression in the people around us and to mirror these. You can think of them as sending signals to your body to copy what you see, and the feedback from your body tells other parts of your brain about what those movements and expressions feel like. In this way, you can almost literally read a person's mind and feel what they are feeling. You can empathise. This is a deep form of understanding, and just what someone in distress needs.

Listening

When we listen, we do so at different levels at different times. These levels range from shallow and superficial to deep and intense.

Pretending

Have you ever just pretended to be listening, because you knew it was expected of you, but you didn't really care about what was being said? Of course you have – how recently? This is just a form of deceit and downright rude. It is no use to anyone.

Selecting

You will also certainly be familiar with your ability to take part in one conversation while subtly eavesdropping on a conversation nearby; perhaps a relative calls in the middle of a radio programme you were listening to. You are more than pretending to listen to them on the phone; your brain is paying some attention so that, when they say something important, you can phase out from the radio and into the phone conversation. You are selecting.

This is perhaps our default mode: we are selecting all the time. Even when we are only part of one conversation, we are selecting between it and that voice in our head that makes a running commentary on what we see and hear; it criticises and judges, it prepares our next statement or response. Consequently, we don't always hear what the other person really says: we were listening to ourselves instead.

This is not good in many ways when listening to someone in distress. First, they will be able to tell that you are not paying full attention and, second, you will inevitably miss something important. But most essential, remember what we said about your first response: don't judge or criticise, don't offer advice, don't probe. These are exactly what that voice in your head will do, instinctively, if you let it. We'll examine how to shut that voice off soon.

Attending

At the next level of listening, you pay full attention to the other person. You focus on them and hear everything they say, giving appropriate and supportive feedback like eye contact, nods or an 'aha' at the right moment. When they finish what they are saying, you may ask another question, and sometimes you will make notes to help you remember things that are important. This is high-quality listening, it is good for gathering information, and is entirely appropriate to most workplace and business meetings and discussions. So what else could there be?

Empathising

When we listen to empathise, we don't just hear what is said; we hear what is not said: we *'listen between the lines'*. Empathising is whole-body listening, where you pay total attention to the other person and start to feel a sense of what they are feeling. You will understand what they are saying in a way that goes far beyond the meaning of their words. This is particularly important for someone in distress, because that very emotional state means that they are unlikely to express themselves especially well in language: they may muddle and confuse words, and you need to follow what they are feeling rather than what they are saying.

> empathising is whole-body listening

How to listen deeply

Listening is a skill and, like all skills, if you follow a good process and practise it, you can get better. Try these six steps out with friends and family and notice what difference your better-quality listening makes to the way they regard you.

Open questions, supportive responses

Listening starts with good questions. These are questions that encourage people to talk about what is important to them, so make your questions open and avoid phrasing them in such a way that they imply the answer you want to hear. Examples of open questions are: *'How do you feel?'* or *'What would you like to talk about?'*

There is one open question to avoid when you are listening to someone who is stressed: *'Why...?'* Whether you intend it to or not, a 'why' question will usually come across as critical or judgemental. If it is important for you to understand why I did something, for example, then find a way to ask your question without the provocative 'why' word; for example: *'When you ... what were your reasons?'* or *'How did you make the decision to...?'*

Having asked a good question, listen to the answer and offer supportive responses. Keep eye contact, lean in appropriately, nod your head, and make small comments like *'I understand,'* *'Yes, I see'* or *'Thank you.'*

Avoid trying to tell the other person how they should feel: *'Oh, that must have been awful.'* It seems like an empathetic way to respond, but you risk misreading their feelings. If your presumption is wrong, even slightly, you risk breaking your rapport or, worse, alienating them. It is far better to ask them how they feel or felt: *'Oh, how did you feel about that?'*

Put yourself out of the way

You are an independent thinker; you have your own ideas, beliefs, opinions, values, and even prejudices. If you want to listen respectfully, then none of these has a place in your listening. If you filter what you hear through your own values and beliefs, you will inevitably find yourself placing a value on what you hear as either: good or bad, right or wrong, sensible or stupid. What you hear is the other person's reality and what you think of it should not be a part of your listening process.

put all of your ideas, prejudices and opinions to one side

Put all of your ideas, prejudices and opinions to one side. A good way to do this is to imagine them all encapsulated in a little version of you: your own 'mini-me'. In your mind's eye, imagine putting that little you right in the far corner of the room or, if you are outside, right to the edge of where you are. See them grow smaller, as they go off to that far place, where they are out of earshot and can't judge what you hear.

Turn off the voice inside

Now you need to turn off that inner dialogue that constantly prepares the next thing you are going to say, thus drowning out what you should be hearing. Don't worry about not being prepared with the right comment or next question: we'll tackle that in a little bit. Imagine your inner voice being controlled by an electronic amplifier, with a big volume knob. In your mind, turn that dial down and down and down until that voice goes silen ...

Become aware of your listening

As you listen, be aware of your listening; are you paying total attention? If that inner voice has started up, turn it down. If you feel yourself criticising or judging, push yourself further away. Is your body still? If you feel yourself fidgeting, then stop. If you are not turned completely towards the other person, turn to them.

brilliant tip

To stop your hands fidgeting, use a meditation technique. If you are sitting, place your right hand in your lap, palm up, with your left hand on top, also palm up. If you are standing, place your right hand just in front of you or behind your back, and lightly hold your left hand. If you are left-handed, reverse this.

We tend to fidget most with our dominant hand, so, here, you are using your other hand to subdue it.

Match and mirror

To get that deep sense of rapport that allows you to really feel what the other person is saying, start to match their posture. Do not simply mimic every aspect, but, rather, match a few key aspects. If you do not have a close personal relationship, avoid mirroring them, so that your left side copies their right, so they see you as they would see themselves in a mirror. Instead, match their left with your left and their right with your right. Mirroring is far more intimate and will be unsettling if that intimacy is inappropriate. Matching facial expressions will give you the most direct insight into their emotions, so notice a frown and try it on, observe a closing of one eye and test it out. You may be amazed at how powerfully you can start to understand what is going on in someone's head.

Reflect, not rephrase

Use the matching and mirroring process with words too, to show you really understand. Pick up on key phrases and play them back verbatim. Do not be tempted to paraphrase them, because your version may not mean exactly the same to them as theirs, and you will appear to them to have misunderstood.

If you know a phrase was important, but you are not sure exactly what it did mean, repeat it back and then test your understanding by rephrasing it in your words and asking if that is a good way to understand what they said. Here's an example.

'I feel like the whole thing is caving in on top of me.'

'The whole thing is caving in on top of you.
Is it that your work feels out of control?'

'Sort of, but it's not just my work; it's everything …
… it's my home life too. It feels like it's crushing me.'

'Ah, everything.
You're feeling crushed; is that like you can't move under it all?'

'Yes, that's exactly it.'

The power of silence

If you turn off your inner voice, you won't be able to prepare your next question or response in advance, because you will be listening. This is good. To prepare your response, you will need to wait until they have stopped speaking and then take a moment to do so. This silence is phenomenally powerful and, when you feel comfortable with it, you will become a far better listener and helper.

First, the silence indicates that you are thinking and therefore tells the other person that what they said is important to you – it is respectful. Secondly, silence is uncomfortable, so they may just fill it. By this time they have said what they consciously wanted to say, and with their guard a little lower they may just tell you something more. This might be really important.

Learn to cultivate silences, because in them lies the truth.

Helping someone to regain control

People need to find their own solutions, so helping is not always about having the answers or offering to do things. Sometimes it is entirely about letting them think through their problem and see it from a new perspective, and then endorsing their own solutions. Remember the essence of this book: any solution that

I find allows me to do something for myself and so it gives me back some control.

This section is not about training you to be a coach, a counsellor or a therapist. But there is a simple five-stage questioning process that will help you to challenge somebody's faulty thinking and restore a sense of control over their life. It's as simple as ABCDE, in fact. We saw Albert Ellis's ABC model towards the end of Chapter 6. We are going to revisit it, and extend it.

A: Activating event

First, enquire into what thing (or things) triggered the feelings of stress. Remember to use the terms that they use for their stress, such as 'overwhelmed', 'stuck', or 'can't cope'. Listen to their description and focus in on some of the things they appear to believe are true, which may not be.

B: Beliefs

Next, actually ask about the beliefs they have about the event, which set off their stress, fears and subsequent responses.

C: Consequences

Then look at the consequences those beliefs had for them. How did they react and what happened next? What you need to help them recognise is that it is their beliefs that have led to the stress response, rather than the activating event itself.

D: Dispute

Now is the time to challenge their beliefs – the faulty thinking that has led them to feel stress in their situation. What is the evidence for their interpretations? What alternative interpretations are possible? How would the alternatives change the way they see the world? And how would things turn out differently, if they act in the future on new beliefs?

E: Energise

The final step is to energise them to do something different: to seize control. In the more conventional therapeutic language, they will exchange old behaviours for new, more empowering ones. This is where you need to be firm, and hold them in some way to account for making at least one small change. This is the first step to taking control and with it will come a sense of victory that will further energise them – especially if you are able to acknowledge it and congratulate them.

Ways to challenge faulty thinking

The D for Dispute step is where the change really starts to take place, so it is worth cataloguing some of the typical ways people can pick up and then articulate false beliefs, and therefore how you can challenge them by asking good-quality questions.

Assigning cause

One of the commonest types of faulty thinking – and one that we are almost compelled to do – is to assign a cause to every event: *'This happened because of that, because of him, because of you.'* Rarely is life as easy. Certainly things do happen for a reason, but encourage the person you are helping to challenge evidence that their reasoning is correct and either find a new, more helpful reason or, perhaps more useful, accept that things just happen and deal with the consequences, rather than worrying about a reason they cannot change.

Assigning meaning

'When she says this, it means she thinks ...' or *'When this happens it means that I am ...'* How can they know what she thinks and what does an external event really tell us about ourselves? Meaning is another thing our brains desperately seek and, again, you need to help the person see that the evidence for their faulty thinking is either absent or flimsy at best.

Reading minds

We all think things like: *'He doesn't think I can cope with this,'* but when we are stressed, we can't just set those thoughts aside as idle speculation. Where is the evidence that he thinks that? What else might he think?

Value judgements

'I'll never be good enough unless I ...' is an example of one of the dangerous attitudes we saw in Chapter 5. But who says so? This kind of faulty thinking sets up expectations of ourselves that nobody has expressed. Another thing you may hear is: *'They say I'll never be good enough unless I ...'* Here, there is a mysterious they, but no more evidence that the value judgement is valid.

Must, Mustn't and Can't

All of these injunctions and assessments of ourselves are mere generalisations. Ask the person whom you are helping to justify their assertions, by testing them out: *'What if you did, or didn't or could?' 'How do you know you must, or mustn't or can't?' 'What compels you, what prevents you?'* Look for what is causing these beliefs and find counter evidence to free them from the strait-jacket of compulsion or inability.

More or less

'I need to work harder' or *'I want less pressure'* are examples of comparisons with an unspecified standard. It will give them more control to set absolute levels of performance, like *'I need to put in eight good solid work hours each day next week'* or *'I want to be able to leave work and feel I can go out with friends on a Friday night, rather than worry about my workload.'*

Accentuating the negative

As the song says, it always helps to eliminate the negative and accentuate the positive, but we do precisely the opposite when we feel down, so your job is to help them focus on what is good, what resources they have, and how things can turn out positively. This has a close relative …

The end is nigh

When we are stressed and unable to think clearly, the smallest things appear to have the greatest consequence. *'If I don't get this done, she'll … hate me, sack me, leave me.'* Help explore the likely real consequences, so that things can be assigned a realistic priority, and some things can be neglected safely and without remorse.

A related form of faulty thinking – and the opposite of assigning cause – is fortune-telling, seeing a future based on little or no evidence and a lot of faulty beliefs and false inferences. Once again, uncovering the source of these predictions can lead to better assessments of what the real evidence indicates.

My fault

The last of our examples of faulty thinking is to accept blame and feel excessive remorse for things – even when there is no blame at all. Tread carefully here, because stressed people do make mistakes. What is important is not the fault, but the remedy. *'It may be your fault, it may not. If it is, you must apologise. Either way, let's think through what needs to be done and what is the first thing you can do to start to put it right.'*

> what is important is not the fault, but the remedy

Blame and reason

'My fault' is one start of the blame game, which turns the blame in on ourself. Another start is to turn the blame on someone else. Now, when we are stressed, we can start to build a whole fantasy on this faulty belief. The psychological field of Transactional Analysis (or TA) has a powerful model that can help you understand what is going on. It is called *The Drama Triangle* and was developed by Stephen Karpman.

The drama triangle

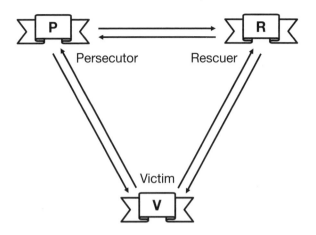

Figure 10.1 The drama triangle

In this triangle, there are three roles: the victim, the persecutor and the rescuer. You are likely to observe two sides of the triangle in place: the person you are helping as the victim and the person they blame as the persecutor. The most important thing to know is this: the drama triangle represents faulty thinking. Victim, persecutor and rescuer roles are perceptions only.

Therefore, you are not there to become their rescuer. If you do, you become part of the drama and risk making the situation worse for them and for you. Let me give you an example of how easily this can happen.

Virgil: *It's so awful; Patsy has given me so much work. I can't cope. I am never going to be able to get home tonight. My weekend will be ruined.*

  (= I am the poor victim here and Patsy is my persecutor.)

Rene: *I am sure Patsy did not mean to ruin your weekend. Let's talk it through.*

(= Patsy is not persecuting you; don't be a victim.)

Virgil: *She may not have meant it, but she's so thoughtless. Thank you for offering to help. I am sure with both of us working on it it'll get done more quickly.*
(= Patsy is persecuting me, but now you have come to rescue me.)

Rene: *I'm sorry, I am not able to stay late with you, but I would be willing to help you plan your work, to get it done more efficiently.*
(= I am not your rescuer.)

Virgil: *I see. You're just like Patsy. Now you want to make me stay late and do Patsy's work. Some friend!*
(= No, you are not my rescuer, you're here to persecute me.)

Rene: *Now hold on. Don't cast me as the bad cop. I only offered to help.*
(= Oh thanks. Now you're persecuting me. I feel like the victim here.)

It would be easy to go on, but you get the drift. These switches around the triangle give us a psychological pay-off, as we shed blame from ourselves and hand it to someone else. We feel good when we rescue and, strangely, feel less responsible when we are victim. When we consciously persecute, we feel in control.

Break the triangle – refuse to get involved in the drama. This is difficult and requires that you can sense a trap and not fall into it. But even then, we saw Rene spot the rescuer trap and still end up feeling persecuted. There are seven ways that can help you avoid stepping on to the drama triangle.

1 Stick to asking questions to uncover facts. With facts, the drama starts to weaken.

2 Invite the other player to take responsibility for themselves.

3   Do nothing to endorse another player's perceptions of themself or of other players.

4   Remain courteous and calm at all times, and pause so you can analyse the perceptions before making a response. Use the SCOPE process.

5   Break the cycle by declaring what is happening. Encourage other players to analyse the drama.

6   Step out of the play. If all else fails, walk away.

7   Refuse to feel bad about how the other player perceives you. Be confident of your own motivations and accept that, if you did not play the situation as you would have wished, then at least you tried in good faith.

Expert help

Pointing someone towards the right professional or expert help is the ultimate way you can help them. Often a GP is a good first port of call, and an appointment will never be the wrong thing for someone whose health is in danger. GPs can help access the full range of social or medical care resources available locally. They will be able to weigh up a full range of options from counselling to therapy to medical help and treatment with prescription drugs.

Here are a few further sources of help you might refer to.

brilliant resources

Sources of professional help

- If you have alcohol-related problems, Alcoholics Anonymous is a good source of help: **www.alcoholics-anonymous.org.uk**

- British Association for Counselling & Psychotherapy (BACP): **www.bacp.co.uk**

▶

- For practical help with legal, financial or other problems, the Citizens' Advice Bureau, CAB: **www.citizensadvice.org.uk**

- Gamblers Anonymous: **www.gamblersanonymous.org.uk**

- International Stress Management Association (ISMA): **www.isma.org.uk**

- For advice relating to mental health, Mind: **www.mind.org.uk**

- For stress with relationships, Relate: **www.relate.org.uk**

- For someone to listen, The Samaritans: **www.samaritans.org**

brilliant recap

- There are four levels of listening and we help best when we commit to the deepest level: empathising.

- Good listening is a learnable skill, so turn off your inner voice, refrain from criticising, and give me your full attention.

- Use Albert Ellis's ABCDE process to help restore a sense of control.

- Don't encourage or allow yourself to get caught up in the blame game. It is futile and destructive.

Relax: last words on stress

Karoshi is a Japanese word (properly transliterated to 'karoushi'):

過労死

Karoshi is usually translated as *'death from overwork'*. It represents a phenomenon well known in 1980s and 1990s Japan. Don't let it happen to you. As we mentioned in Chapter 5, nobody ever said as their dying words, *'I wish I'd spent more time on my work.'*

Relax

Imagine that all the stresses in your life are like a wind blowing around you. And you, sitting where you are, are like a strong powerful tree, with all the ideas and resources you have gathered from this book. As the wind blows, you are confident that your roots are deep and you are strong and supple. You laugh at the puny attempts of the wind to blow you over. You look up to the ceiling and you smile to yourself and you feel your roots stretch downwards, anchoring you to solid ground.

You may sway in the wind, the gales may ruffle your leaves, but whatever comes, you know you are strong. Whatever happens now, stay focused on who you are, what is most important to you, and what you have to be grateful for. Whatever comes, meet it calmly.

And enjoy.

Appendix 1

101 ways to reduce your stress

1 Tell yourself you're doing well.

2 Exercise regularly.

3 Make time to relax.

4 A hot bath.

5 A hot shower.

6 Reduce your caffeine.

7 Eat well.

8 Meditation.

9 Sleep.

10 Set goals.

11 Celebrate each little success.

12 Be optimistic about the future.

13 Better time management.

14 Do the things you *must* do.

15 Abandon the things you *should* do.

16 Do more of the things you *want* to do.

17 Play with your children.

18 Play with your friends.

19 Play with yourself.

20 Treat yourself to something nice.

21 Simplify your life.

22 Tidy your desk.

23 Clear out clutter.

24 Go to a comedy show.

25 Watch your favourite movie.

26 Count your blessings (literally).

27 Forgive someone.

28 Breathe deeply.

29 Drink more water.

30 Stop beating yourself up.

31 Pamper yourself.

32 Make love with your partner.

33 Buy yourself a present.

34 Volunteer to help others with more serious problems.

35 Say thank you when you go shopping.

36 Say thank you to machines.

37 Say hello to your colleagues.

38 Listen to music.

39 Smile.

40 Get a pet.

41 Eat some chocolate.

42 Get a massage.

43 Go for a walk.

44 Take the phone off the hook.

45 Leave work early one day.

46 Say 'no' and feel good about it.

47 Go swimming.

48 Set up a squash, tennis, darts match with a friend.

49 Walk to the pub and chat with the people there.

50 Dig the garden and plant some seeds.

51 Arrange a weekend away.

52 Go to a café, order a drink, and watch the world go by.

53 Call a friend and have a chat.

54 Take a walk and pay attention to the colours, the plants and any birds and animals you see, hear or smell.

55 Prepare for tomorrow.

56 Transfer items from your To Do list to your To Don't list.

57 Turn down the lighting.

58 Have an early night.

59 Make a nice and healthy meal.

60 Take a day off from stimulants like caffeine, alcohol and television.

61 Curl up with a good book.

62 Go out to lunch with one or two good friends.

63 Control your urge to be strong and independent, and ask for help.

64 Make some time to laugh during the day – chat at the coffee machine.

65 Read a funny novel or buy a copy of *Dilbert*, *Far Side* or *Calvin and Hobbes*.

66 Let go of any grudges or resentments towards any colleagues.

67 Replace chocolate snacks with fruit or even vegetables like carrots and celery.

68 When you eat, pay close attention to the smell, taste and texture of your food.

69 '*I should have*' is a major cause of stress – if it's important, do it; if it's not, then let it go!

70 Try out a new non-sporting form of exercise: yoga, tai chi, Pilates, Chi Kung, Aikido, Alexander, Shiatsu …

71 Join a dance class or club.

72 Turn on some music at home and just dance like no one is watching. It's best to make sure no one is watching.

73 Get a manicure or pedicure, or facial.

74 Get some toys and play with them.

75 Plan a great holiday.

76 Create and use a positive, de-stressing, self-affirming mantra.

77 Learn advanced techniques for managing your mental state, such as CBT or NLP.

78 Turn off your email.

79 Turn off your computer.

80 Have a lie-in in the morning.

81 Take a break from the news – avoid papers, television or radio news and Internet news services.

82 Ask yourself: '*How important will this seem, this time next year?*'

83 Pay compliments to the people you meet.

84 Eat more fruit.

85 Have a good stretch.

86 Take a nap.

87 Set aside some time for silence – sit quietly and close your eyes.

88 Eat more nuts and seeds.

89 Have a good breakfast.

90 Savour the moment and focus on experiencing what you are seeing, hearing, feeling, smelling and tasting *now*.

91 Start to value your time as your most precious commodity.

92 Confide in a friend and share your stresses and strains with them.

93 Take a break – in fact, schedule regular five-minute breaks into your work pattern.

94 Make sure you have half an hour of time to yourself each day.

95 Plan what you will do on your weekends so you will use them well.

96 Re-read the 'Relax' section on page 201.

97   Go out to a concert or a play.

98   Take yourself to somewhere beautiful and spend time admiring the view – especially at that golden hour around dawn or dusk.

99   Take a day or even a week off and go away somewhere spontaneously.

100   Have a nice cup of tea and a biscuit.

101   And relax.

Appendix 2

Learn more

There are organisations that can help at various points in this book. Here, there are some further books you could read.

Books on stress and stress management

Clegg, B. (2000) *Instant Stress Management: bring calm to your life now*. Kogan Page.

Cunningham, J.B. (2000) *The Stress Management Sourcebook*. McGraw Hill.

Quick, J.C. and Cooper, C.L. (2003) *Stress and Strain*. Fast Facts. Health Press Limited.

Sapolsky, R.M. (2004) *Why Zebras don't get ulcers: an updated guide to stress, stress-related diseases, and coping*. Saint Martin's Press Inc.

Books on positive psychology

ben-Shahar, T. (2008) *Happier: can you learn to be happy?* McGraw Hill Professional.

Emmons, R.A. (2008) *Thanks! How practising gratitude can make you happier*. Houghton Mifflin Company.

Seligman, M.E.P. (2003) *Authentic Happiness: using the new positive psychology to realize your potential for lasting fulfilment*. Nicholas Brealey.

Seligman, M.E. (2006) *Learned Optimism: how to change your mind and your life.* Vintage Books.

Books on particular topics

Back, K. and Back, K. (2005) *Assertiveness at Work, a practical guide to handling awkward situatioins.* McGraw Hill Professional.

Briers, S. (2009) *Brilliant Cognitive Behavioural Therapy.* Prentice Hall.

Clayton, M. (2010) *Brilliant Time Management.* Prentice Hall.

Clayton, M. (2010) *The Handling Resistance Pocketbook.* Management Pocketbooks.

Lawless, J. (2002) *Complete Illustrated Guide to Aromatherapy: a practical approach to the use of essential oils for health and well-being.* Element.

Macdonald, G. (1998) *The Complete Illustrated Guide to Alexander Technique: a practical programme for health, poise, and fitness.* Element.

Martin, P. (2010) *Counting Sheep: the science and pleasures of sleep and dreams.* Flamingo.

McGilvery, C. *et al.* (2010) *The Stressbusting Book of Yoga, Massage and Aromatherapy.* Southwater.

Stewart, I. and Joines, V. (1987) *TA Today: a new introduction to Transactional Analysis.* Lifespace Publishing.

Tohei, K. (2001) *Ki in Daily Life.* Japan Publications Trading Co.

Website

www.brilliantstressmanagement.com

Index